the journey

the journey

ABDUL MUSA ADAM
with Ros Wynne-Jones

MIRROR BOOKS

First published by Mirror Books in 2020

Mirror Books is part of Reach plc
10 Lower Thames Street
London EC3R 6EN

www.mirrorbooks.co.uk

ISBN 978-1-912624-24-9

Typeset by Danny Lyle

Printed and bound in Great Britain by
CPI Group (UK) Ltd, Croydon, CR0 4YY

A CIP catalogue record for this book is available from the British Library.

1 3 5 7 9 10 8 6 4 2

Cover images: Getty

For Yusuf

"You know how you let yourself think that everything will be all right if you can only get to a certain place or do a certain thing. But when you get there you find it's not that simple."

Richard Adams, *Watership Down*

Foreword
by Lord Dubs

No two refugee stories are the same. But there are themes that are common to all of them, the most striking of which, counterintuitive as it may sound, is luck.

For me the luck came when my mother was able to secure me a place on the kindertransport, aged six, which meant I was able to flee the Nazis, who had invaded my home town of Prague. My dad escaped almost immediately after the Germans occupied Prague in March 1939, and so I was also lucky to have been one of the few children who was met off the kindertransport at Liverpool Street station by a parent – while many of the 10,000 children who arrived on the kindertransport were welcomed by strangers.

Luckier still, my mum was also able to escape and join my father and me in London. That stroke of luck rested on the shoulders of the German soldier who refused her permission to leave Czechoslovakia, but after throwing her down the stairs of the office where she had requested that permission, threw her passport after her, which meant she could somehow find a way out of the country.

It could have been so different. The friends and family we left behind in Prague all fled, or were unable to flee and perished in the death camps.

Despite the awful tragedies Abdul endured, Abdul was lucky too. His life opportunities turned on the toss of a coin, arriving as he did in a community where his skills of horsemanship were valued and he was welcomed. The coin, that time at least, fell in his favour.

There are other parallels between my refugee story and Abdul's. Although our homes and communities were both ravaged by genocide and we both lost our families, I detect that we both find some kind of solace and peace in the stillness of walking the British countryside.

I love hill and mountain walking. I love the colours and contours of the British landscape. I've always thought that at 1,000 feet our problems seem small, at 2,000 feet they are tiny and at 3,000 feet those problems can almost disappear.

I can also sense in Abdul's story the same grateful love for the UK that I have felt passionately all my life. There is a unique and special kind of respect and love that I believe only a refugee can feel for the country that adopts them. Like Abdul, the UK gave me a chance to have a life, for which I will be forever grateful. We've also both met the Queen.

But in crucial ways our stories also diverge. We may have both come here as unaccompanied refugee children, but in comparison to Abdul's story, mine was a walk in the park.

It took me two days to reach safety in the UK. The wooden seats we sat on were hard, but it was hardly any great sufferance to sleep on those. I was warm, I was surrounded by other children.

When we reached the Dutch border, the older children cheered. I didn't know why – I was busy looking out for clogs and windmills – but I had a sense that we were safe. Before I left Prague, my mother packed me a knapsack of food for the journey, which I delivered to my dad, untouched, when I arrived. Hunger was never part of my story.

Abdul took seven years to arrive. The details of his journey are nothing short of harrowing. He lost his parents, he was tortured, exploited and endured unbearable suffering. That he, a child alone in the world, also felt an additional huge weight of responsibility for his brother, is a situation I can't imagine.

I arrived by train, Abdul on the underside of a truck. No two refugee stories are the same, but what Abdul endured is beyond my comprehension.

There are two remarkable people behind this book. It is, of course, Abdul's story, and what an inspiring and hope-filled story it is, and what an impressive young man he has become. But that story would never have been told were it not for Ros Wynne-Jones, who wrote his story down.

What people perhaps forget about refugee children is that being a refugee disrupts everything, including, crucially, education. Even if a refugee child is lucky enough to find a new home, the years of missed schooling are hard to replace – the refugee years cast a long shadow.

For Abdul that shadow means he cannot read or write. So, for Ros to be able to tell his story, every page she wrote had to be carefully and painstakingly read back to Abdul, with the help of an Arabic translator, to make sure the story really is in his words.

Ros is no stranger to the suffering of refugees. Early in her career as a journalist she covered the Rwandan genocide and later the brutal realities of life in the Darfuri refugee camps inside Eastern Chad, which is ultimately how she came to know Abdul. Stories like Abdul's can only be told with the help of people like Ros. And they must be told, because they reveal the very worst, but also the very best in our humanity.

Foreword

I am privileged to have been asked to write this introduction. I am grateful to the people of Wiltshire for giving Abdul a home, to the UK for allowing his skills and talents to flourish here to the benefit of his adopted country, and to all those who make refugees welcome.

Alf Dubs, House of Lords, January 2020

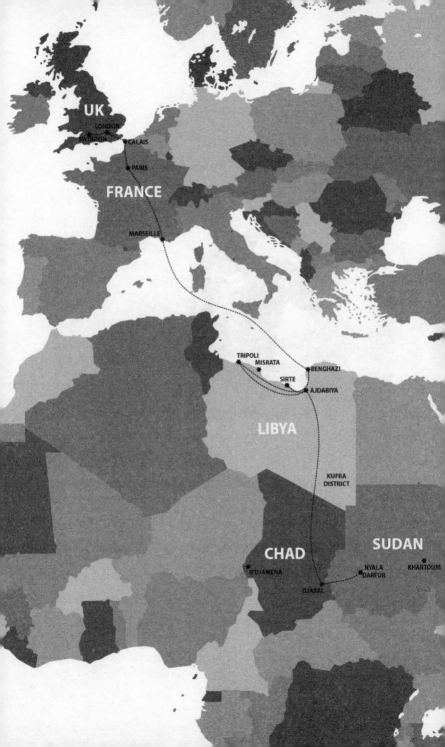

Prologue
Kingsclere

It's almost lunchtime, but I can tell King's Lynn doesn't want to come in as I lead him back towards the stables. The conditions on the chalk downs are almost perfect, the autumn turf springy under his hooves. The bright sunshine has warmed the ground along the gallops, and the rain has washed the air fresh and clean again. The birds are shouting at us as we cross the meadow.

I pull King's Lynn towards the outdoor shower and take off his blanket and saddle. Sweat covers the deep brown of his back. I watch the colt shiver as the water hits. As I dry him off, I give him an apple I pocketed at breakfast, and he rubs his soft nose into my hand.

King's Lynn is two years old, a bay horse with a dark brown mane and a distinctively wide white stripe down his nose. He is the son of two legendary horses, Kinetic and Cable Bay. He's not just royal by name, but by owner, because he belongs to Her Majesty the Queen.

I watch the horse's strong teeth crunch on the apple. I can tell a lot about a horse just by handling them, and I can feel King's Lynn is a bit on edge today. I have been riding for almost 20 years, since the age of two. I can tell if an animal is sick or if something is bothering them.

I always feel the most connected to my family when I am with horses. It's hard to explain, but when I touch a horse, I feel my mother and father's spirits are there. I feel calm and relaxed and in some way at home, even though my real home is 3,000 miles away in Darfur.

My life since becoming a refugee in the UK has been shaped by one piece of luck. That the lorry I clung underneath to come to England happened to make its first stop just north of the North Wessex Downs, a landscape with such a strong relationship to horses and riding that it has a string of white horses etched into the chalk.

King's Lynn is on edge because he knows he's got a big race on Saturday. The Queen will come to see his jockey wear her colours at Doncaster: purple, scarlet and gold. She knows about horses. She had her first horse, Peggy, a Shetland Pony, at the age of four. I could already ride a big stallion by that age, and I could ride a camel, and I knew how to herd sheep and goats.

I think King's Lynn knows he is a Royal horse, and he knows that my grandfather was the leader of a tribe of nomads. Perhaps I would have become a leader myself one day in Sudan, but instead I am here, a Rider Groom at a famous stables in England, a place that only existed in my grandfather's stories when I was a child.

Before the race I will brush beautiful markings into King's Lynn's quarters that will show how strong and handsome he is. It will help him to win. Sometimes I make the markings of my tribe. If I took off my shirt you would see them all across my back, a ring of 25 lines. In Darfur, when you are child, you are marked with sharp sticks, scars that show who you belong to, and what your status is. Like a passport, they say I am a Darfuri, which sheikh, which dialect. We don't have villages because we are nomads, but we carry our history on our skin. I carry other marks too from my childhood journey to the UK through three war zones and under a lorry. Those scars are part of my skin's history too.

I lead the Queen's horse back to his red-brick stable, one of more than 50 which open onto several yards. I pick out his hooves, which are full of mud and straw under his work shoes, and strap a clean blanket on his back to keep him warm. I feed him some hay and he tries to bite my hand, in a friendly way. He sniffs the pocket of my fleece in the hope of another apple.

Racehorses need to rest in the afternoons after hard riding in the mornings, so I close up the stable, and cross the yard to walk back to the house. A radio is playing loudly in one of the other stables, and I can hear the ching-ching of the farrier at work shoeing a horse.

In the middle of the yard is a giant bronze statue of Mill Reef, one of the greatest racehorses that ever lived. I like to look at the statue as I walk past. It says that he won Horse of the Year in England, 1971. He was trained by my boss Andrew Balding's father Ian. Because of Mill Reef, our uniform is black and gold. His owner left the colours to Kingsclere when he died.

In Darfur, my family used to race horses too. There would be races at weddings, at Eid, when a woman gives birth, when a boy is circumcised. Men would race horses and camels, the way they once rode them to conquer lands, with the skills passed on from father to son, at huge gatherings that bring the clans together. We rode bareback in Darfur through clouds of red dust, with only turbans to cover our heads and stop the sand from getting into our eyes.

I'm thinking of all this as I take everything to the washing machines to wash, and so at first I don't hear Andrew's wife Anna Lisa, who keeps a close eye on all of us, calling me.

"Abdul!" she says. "How was today? Will you take Tonto for a walk?"

Tonto is Anna Lisa's giant boxer dog. I love taking him for a walk. I grew up walking long distances, and it clears my head. It helps me to relax and think about things. For a long time, I didn't like dogs, but Tonto is a friend.

"Yes," I say.

I grab my lunch to take with me, and walk up to Park House, along the gravel path, to collect the dog. It's a magnificent house with columns outside the front door and long, wide windows, surrounded by trees and perfect lawns. I've taken off my riding hat but I'm still wearing my jodhpurs and my jacket. I keep my riding boots on because it's muddy today. Tonto is a beautiful dog, huge, like a horse. He's waiting for me at the back door, so I don't need to take my boots off. We cut back around the side of the house and then up into the changing autumn treeline, through the fields to the chalk Downs where King's Lynn and I rode the gallops earlier.

The trees are heavy with late fruit, and birds are circling the track looking for grubs dug up by the horses' hooves. The white lanes we train along stand out against the bright green of the grass and the churned brown of the mud. Only half an hour ago, I was thundering along there myself, watching the landscape I'm standing on now fly past me in a blur of brown, green and orange. At this time of year, the bay of the horses blends in perfectly with the colours around them, with the changing leaves and with the horse chestnuts they are crushing underfoot.

Tonto and I push on beyond the track, up towards the beautiful Watership Down, the place I loved before I knew the story of the rabbits, and that I have loved even more ever since. Their story is also my story. Young rabbits searching their world for somewhere safe to live, but finding again and again that the place where they have settled is not safe and they must push on again in search of freedom.

Up on the top, I can see for miles, all the way to Beacon Hill in the distance. When I walk here with Tonto in the evenings or at first light, I see all kinds of creatures – roe deer, lapwings, bats, skylarks. Sometimes you see red kites riding on the air thermals or green woodpeckers scrubbing for ants, or linnets and goldfinches in winter. You see hares, and, of course, rabbits. Tonto always spots them first.

As I reach the top this lunchtime, I see an unusual sight. A blue-coloured dome, stranded in the middle of the grass. It's made of shiny material. It looks like aliens have landed on the Downs. It's shaped like a mosque.

As I get closer, I realise it's a tent. This is very exciting to me. I was born in a tent. I've never seen people living in a tent in England, though. And then something even more curious happens. A white man comes out. A white man in a tent – Abdul you've seen it all, I think to myself.

I walk straight towards him with Tonto and wave to him.

"What do you want?" the man says.

He doesn't seem friendly. He's about the same age as me, I think. 21. I can see two bicycles next to the tent. He keeps looking from me to Tonto. I think we are an unusual sight: a boy from Darfur in jodhpurs and riding boots and a massive, oversized boxer dog. He doesn't know Tonto wouldn't hurt a fly.

"Excuse me," I say. "Could I look inside your tent?"

"Look inside?" the man repeats, blocking my path with his body. "I shouldn't think so, no!"

"I'd really like to see inside," I say. "I was born in a tent. I haven't even seen a tent for years. Are you nomads? Do you live here now?"

The man is quite red in the face now.

"Look, piss off, mate," he says.

Tonto pulls his ears back. He's not impressed with this man.

"You should be the one to piss off," I say. "This is my boss's field. I am a jockey at Park House Stables. I'm allowed to be here."

I can feel Tonto's annoyance next to me.

As we're speaking, another man suddenly appears. I think he must have been inside the tent. He has a friendlier face than the first man.

"Where are you from?" the second man asks me.

"I come from Darfur, in Sudan," I say. "But I lost my whole family. When I saw the tent, I felt happy, that's why I came to talk to you."

The first man looks embarrassed.

"What would you like to see?" the second man says, leading the way into the tent.

Their tent is really funny inside. It doesn't have a pole in the middle. It has chairs inside and two mattresses full of air. It's quite messy.

"What do you think, then?" the first man asks.

"It's not a very good tent," I tell him. "It's too small. It wouldn't be very good in a sandstorm. And the bed is too small. Our bed used to sleep my mother, my father, my sisters, my brother and me."

The men look at each other for a moment, then they burst out laughing.

"What's your name, mate?" the first man says.

"Abdul," I say.

"That's a long journey you've been on," he says.

I look at him. It's a very obvious thing to say.

Their names are John and Adam and they come from the north of England. They are walking and riding their bicycles around the country, camping in between.

"You're right, we should have asked your boss's permission to camp here," Adam says. "We were looking for Watership Down. We'll only be here a night."

"Well, you are like nomads, then," I say.

By the time I leave them, it's already past lunchtime and I've forgotten to eat my lunch.

"Bye Abdul!" they shout, and they are my friends now.

Walking back, I feel happy to have seen the tent, but I feel a very heavy sadness too. Seeing the inside made me think of my mum and dad, and my sisters Sharifa and Amina and my brother Yusuf. Usually when I walk Tonto, I feel better, but tonight I know I'm going to be having one of those nights when I don't sleep at all, and all the images keep playing across my mind, like a television you can't switch off.

This is not good. The next 24 hours are really important. King's Lynn is racing. Seeusoon has got a big race all the way out in Norfolk, and then I've got an important appointment of my own. I need to keep very calm and focused, and I need to sleep tonight.

I've been sleeping badly again, the last few weeks. I thought I saw my brother Yusuf on a report from Calais on the television, in the place they call the Jungle. I haven't seen him in 12 years, since he was six and I was 10, and we were in a refugee camp together in Chad. I don't know what he looks like as a 19-year-old man. But there was something about the boy's face that had a look of Yusuf.

Since then I have hardly slept, maybe just three or four hours a night. It tortures me to think Yusuf might be sleeping in a cold tent or on the freezing streets, hungry and frightened, when I am in a warm bed here, well fed and safe at Park House stables. It's a hard thing to explain to people. They think that now I am safe I should feel good and happy. But because Yusuf is not with me, the better things are for me, the worse I feel.

I look at the clock. 2.45pm, and it's already time for Evening Stables, when the horses' boxes need skipping out. I need to feed King's Lynn, Seeusoon and the other horses I'm responsible for and get them ready for the night. I spend the next two hours preparing their beds, feeding and grooming them until their coats are gleaming, and then wrap them in rugs to keep them warm.

Afterwards, I stand with Seeusoon for a while before heading back to the hostel for dinner with the other stable lads and lasses. Stroking his neck, I feel my mother and father's spirits come to me through the horse and through my fingers. Before a big race, it is my job to calm the horses and make sure they feel safe and secure. But this evening I can feel the horse's big heart beating, and it slows my own heart down.

Chapter One
Darfur

This is what I remember, although sometimes I don't know what I remember any more, and other times I remember different versions of the same thing. My memory is shot with holes by trauma, and by how young I was when I made my journey. But the saddest thing is that my memory has no companion. There is no-one to check my story with, because everyone is gone except my little brother Yusuf, and even he can't be found.

I was born in a tent in the handsome district of Kass in Southern Darfur, to a family of nomads of the Zaghawa tribe. We moved in a camp of around 100 people from place to place, wherever there was water or good grazing lands. We would stay a month, or sometimes a few months, in one place. If the grass ran out, or the water dried up, or the herd was unhappy, we moved to another place.

The Journey

I liked it when we all travelled together. I remember very well the women in their beautiful bright dresses of purple, blue and yellow, with pots and baskets balancing on their heads, the men in white guiding the animals, spreading out towards the horizon. Some of the men would have gone on ahead on camels to find the new lands. When we arrived, the first thing we did was light fires. Then, that evening, we would sacrifice an animal and celebrate with food and drink into the night.

Our camp had no school and no doctors. But we had plenty of animals. My family had large herds of cattle, sheep and camels, meaning we were relatively wealthy. When we made camp, we would dig in the ground to make a well for water. We would burn wood and dung to keep off the mosquitos and flies. On clear nights, the sky would be full of stars, so many that you could never count them, and it was never fully dark.

Darfur is not like the empty, dry desert of north Sudan or the red scrubland of South Sudan. In this western part of the country, which juts out like a hip between north and south, pockets of dry scrub and rocky outcrops are interspersed with lush, thick forest, and grasslands fed by riverbeds, where animals graze and the grass grows so green it hurts your eyes.

When the rains had been, we would eat the finest mango, guava, grapes and sweet round oranges straight from the trees. In droughts, my mother and sisters were excellent foragers, finding tiny wild grains and gathering them to eat.

At mealtimes we would roast quail or little black chickens, and if there were celebrations, my father would sometimes catch a gazelle. My favourite food was fufu, boiled cassava pounded into a kind of dough, and we would drink camel milk, which the elders say stops you catching malaria.

My dad had a very naughty monkey called Diggle, who always stayed with him. Sometimes Diggle would fight with me, but my father always took the monkey's side. We had two dogs who worked hard to protect the animals. We had three horses, a mum, a dad, and a foal. I taught my brother to ride the sheep. It made my father angry, but Yusuf and I had to walk a long way to look after the animals, and when he got tired, I used to put him on a sheep and tell him to hold on. It was safer because otherwise if it got too late wild animals would come.

There were a lot of wild animals. Leopards, lions, snakes. Our job was to protect the herd. I used poisoned arrows, but my sister Sharifa had a gun because she was older than me. Sharifa, who was as strong and tough as a man and rode horses and camels better than anyone, was well known in our local area.

One day we were looking after the animals when cattle rustlers approached. I was frightened, but Sharifa was completely calm. As the men approached, she lifted her gun and raised it to her eye, so she could see along the barrel.

"Where are you from, and what do you want?" she asked them.

The men hesitated for a moment, then turned and ran away.

My eldest sister was called Amina. She stayed at home and looked after my mum. She wasn't as fierce as Sharifa. The girls had their lips tattooed with a black line and some special scars on their faces, and both were very beautiful. Amina liked cooking and helping the women. Yusuf was the youngest of all of us, just three years old. He had a sweet nature, shy and a bit nervous. Those were very happy days, living together. I wish I could take that time and just freeze-frame it, a beautiful time before everything that happened.

My family were well known in South Darfur. As well as owning a large number of animals, my grandfather was the local sheikh. I was his favourite grandson, and the closest one to him of all his grandchildren. His name was Adam too – Adam Issa. That's where I get my full name from, Abdulkareem Musa Adam. He was a very peaceful man who wore long white robes, and never had problems with other tribes. He was a holy man, who would officiate at wedding ceremonies, and people would come to him for advice. He was a healer too – if somebody fell off their horse, they would bring them to my grandfather to fix them. And if they had a problem with an animal, my grandfather could speak to the animal too.

My grandfather was a wonderful man who was loved by everybody. He told wonderful stories in our Zaghawa language. When we were together, we always spoke Zaghawa and some other tribal languages but we could all speak Arabic too. Arabic is the language all north Sudanese speak alongside their tribal languages: it's a trading language and allows us nomads to speak to people wherever we go.

At a certain time, every day, my grandfather would call all the children to the camp, whatever religion or household. They would all come quickly for the pile of dates and sweet treats he would have gathered for us all, but also for his stories.

My grandfather had some strong views about religion, which he thought had caused too much fighting in Africa and all over the world.

"You are all one as human beings," he taught us. "Whether Moses or Ibrahim, African Gods or the Muslim prophets, Allah or the Christian God. Do not worry about religions and gods, because in the end, we are all one people. The most important thing is to be a good, brave, kind and decent person. Don't worry about the after-life. Think about now."

I would look forward every day to going to listen to my grandfather. All these years later, and after all my travels, his stories remain very vivid in my mind.

I would always sit at the very front with the dates and sweets and watch his beard moving and his eyes twinkling when he spoke to us.

"There are other people than us," my grandfather would tell us. "I have been to Chad and seen all kinds of men. Even men and women with white skin. White people."

We couldn't believe what we were hearing. All of us began whispering to each other. People with white skin?

"One day you will see them!" my grandfather insisted. "I am old, but you will see them. People with green and blue eyes, who believe in a different God".

We thought he must have gone crazy. What was he talking about?

Sometimes, now, I wonder what my grandfather would think if he could see me today, living with white people and riding their horses in a country 3,000 miles from Darfur.

The best days in Darfur were holidays when a couple were getting married or long-lost visitors arrived from afar. On these days, and others when the different tribes would get together, there would be horse races, as there have been for centuries. My father was one of the best racers in the village, and my sister another.

Like the other men, my father rode with no riding hat. Instead he wore a cloth around his face and nose to keep the dust from choking him. We all often rode bareback, even we little ones, but on race days, my father would use stirrups, and a thick, beautifully stitched blanket instead of a saddle.

Women didn't race, so my sister could never win a competition. Instead she had to lead out the decorated horses at weddings and festivals.

My father taught me to ride. I remember him teaching me when I was a tiny boy, lifting me up onto the smallest horse first of all. I knew immediately I would be a good rider. My father hit the horse gently on its flank and it ran forward, but I didn't fall off. I loved all of our animals. I often slept with them in the tent in the rain or sandstorms. I spent all day with them, talking to them, knowing all their ideas and personalities. But I loved the horses most of all. They had a way of looking at you, and fine, noble faces.

Horses have many different roles in Darfuri culture, and our people are known for being great horsemen and breeders, even obsessively so. Every nomadic group has at least one or two in their herd, and in some tribes, a man is not deemed to be a man unless he owns one. Horses are used to chase off cattle rustlers, to go on missions to look for water or pasture, to travel between towns, and for ceremonial moments like weddings and funerals.

The horses for racing are often descended from other fine racehorses – stretching back to British colonial times, or to horses that escaped from the polo fields and racing stables in Khartoum, the capital of Sudan, or from the Italian-Abyssinian cavalry in Ethiopia. In 1965, a 39-year-old Queen Elizabeth II visited the racecourse at Khartoum on the occasion of her state visit to Sudan.

On big race meets, hundreds, sometimes thousands of Darfuris dressed in white will emerge from the scrub-land to watch the horses over a three or four-day festival. The winners can become wealthy overnight, winning thousands of Sudanese pounds. In the evening, famous singers and poets perform for the audience, and the elders meet in the shade to discuss matters of war and peace.

When you are a child in Darfur there is no school, but there is not much time to play either. Boys look after the animals and girls carry firewood and water and help with the cooking. But while looking after the animals I would climb trees and go swimming in the river during the rains.

Sometimes we would get to play in the clay along the edge of the river making little pottery animals – cows, camels, goats and horses that we would leave to dry in the baking sun. These were our toys, which we had made ourselves. We didn't have toy cars or bicycles, never mind actual cars or bicycles. Sometimes even now when I see a muddy riverbank, I can't help but start scraping out the mud and moulding it. Even now, my windowsill is covered in animals I have never seen in England – elephants and giraffe.

One day, I was out looking after the herd with Yusuf when we saw a white vehicle in the distance with a red cross on it. We were completely amazed, and also frightened to see this metal object coming towards us on four wheels, at such speed, with dust flying behind it. It got nearer until we could see the sun glinting off the glass and metal, but then it turned away towards Gereida, the camp for people displaced by war. For a while we stood and watched it lumber up and down the dry riverbeds until it became a tiny white ant in the distance. We wondered if the people it carried were white people like my grandfather had seen.

Some people said the Red Cross people were there to help you, others that they would be bad for the village.

After that time, there were even more strange sightings. Camels being ridden in packs in the distance by men dressed in white robes and head-dresses. And then, one day, a far off buzz in the air that had us all standing craning our necks with our hands shading our eyes. I saw it first. The white carcass of a tiny aeroplane floating like a buzzard through the searing blue of the sky. A car with wings.

One of my favourite things was to go to the markets with my mother, where women would lay out pieces of cloth on the dry soil and line up their wares grown in the wetter parts of the country. Piles of huge, soft tomatoes and green avocados. Hard lines of onions, sweet potatoes, lemons and limes, and of course the long-fingered okra, which few Darfuri meals are taken without. Thin green chillis separated into neat mountains, each enough for a big stew. Baobab fruit, known as monkey bread for its texture, and baobab bark, which is believed to treat almost any ailment. And the beautiful flowers of hibiscus that can be made into the refreshing, bright red drinks we dreamed of in that dusty heat. The sellers would bargain hard with the women but stuff little piles of groundnuts into the hands of us children, which we would chew on the long journey home to our camp.

That night the women and girls would cook up Darfur's favourite foods. Thick porridge-like aseeda, made from millet or cassava flour, and full of enough energy to sustain even the strongest men of the tribe. In Chad and Libya, we called this fufu. My earliest memories are of the women making the flour, pounding millet or cassava between stones or in a pestle and mortar.

Aseeda would be served with a spicy stew of tomatoes, chilli, okra and beans – or meat or dried fish if it was available. We called this stew "mullah". On special occasions, many other dishes would be added – delicacies made from peanuts blended with sheep's lungs, liver and stomach, bowls of sesame sauces made with garlic, and tangy goat yoghurt spiked with chillis.

Our childhood was never rich, and it was often tough. We worked hard, walked far, slept on hard ground, and never really owned any things. But looking back on it, it was idyllic. We had everything we needed. While war raged below us in South Sudan, to the west of us in Chad, and there were cattle raids and tensions among our tribes, the crimes Khartoum committed against us were largely ones of omission. We were ignored, marginalised and impoverished by our northern neighbours, but not yet exterminated and wiped off our land. If we saw distant aeroplanes, we stopped to stare and wave and wonder at them. We had yet to learn to fear their cargo.

When I was six, my childhood ended, and war came to Darfur. The markets vanished, and in their place were empty stalls, or just thin piles of vegetables laid out on cloth. Irrigation systems were deliberately destroyed, crops burned, livestock stolen, and farmers killed. The pastoralists lived their lives in one place, and either died defending their land or became homeless, wandering destitute until they reached one of the IDP camps for "Internally Displaced Persons".

As herders, we could move if we were attacked. And so, of course, the other thing children had to quickly learn to do in any Darfuri community was look out for the Antonov and the Janjaweed. The Antonovs are the converted Russian-made cargo planes that now carry bombs. They have a distinctive low sound, different from any other, that every child in Sudan knows means to run immediately for cover, shouting for others to do the same. Once you have heard the Antonov, you may only have seconds to get to one of the bomb shelters dug by the community.

Up in the sky, men may already be rolling illegal barrel bombs out through the cargo hatch that are full of shrapnel and high explosives. They are hoping to catch you. Or maybe you are lucky, and they are just doing a recce, ready to come back to bomb you at night.

The Antonovs came from the sky, but the Janjaweed came by land. Their name literally means "man with gun on horse". People also sometimes called them the Baggara, because a lot of Janjaweed fighters come from that tribe. Either way they are a paramilitary force used by the government.

You know when the Janjaweed are coming because you see the dust rising far off in the distance from their camels and horses. And lately they had started coming in military jeeps too, men hanging off the back with rocket launchers. However they came, they arrived in a hail of gunfire, with scarves covering their faces, wrapped up against the dust and the terrible things they had come to do.

Chapter Two
Janjaweed

In the year 2004, when I was seven years old, I was up at our encampment when four jeeps armed with rocket launchers, full of men carrying Kalashnikovs, pulled up. We weren't in any doubt who they were. They were Janjaweed.

Several men in camouflage trousers, black T-shirts and white headdresses jumped off the back of the jeep, carrying their weapons. Some stayed in the vehicle, smoking cigarettes and looking out with bored, reddened eyes at our tents strung together from sticks and colourful fabrics. Even though no shots had been fired, some of the younger children began sobbing and hiding in their mother's skirts, and the women began slipping back towards the encampment. Too many had already experienced the violent assault of the Janjaweed, who always left women alive to rape.

My grandfather was sitting in his usual place in the tent, sipping tea surrounded by the elders, a pile of dates next to him. He got up slowly, and with the grace of an old man, walked across to the jeep. Nobody spoke.

After what seemed a long time, my grandfather reached the man who appeared to be the leader. He was unarmed and leaning on the jeep, his arms folded across his chest and wearing sunglasses. A cigarette, something we had very rarely seen, was burning low between his fingers.

"Old man, tell your people to leave this land," the man said to my grandfather in Arabic.

The children were all mesmerised by the burning cigarette, but my grandfather spoke to them all in a clear, loud voice.

"This is our land, we will not move," he said. "This is where we will stay, and if necessary, this is where we will die."

The man considered this for a moment, before grinding out his cigarette under his boot.

"We have come on government orders," he said. "And you will move. If you refuse to move now, we will come back with the Antonov. It's your choice."

My grandfather asked them to leave so he could discuss the matter with the elders of the tribe. He always believed people should decide together, rather than him tell them what to do. This day was no different.

"I need some time to consult my people," he said. "This is a decision for the whole camp."

It wasn't usual for the Janjaweed to warn people before coming in and destroying their villages, and I don't know if it was because someone somewhere had some respect for my grandfather, or whether they had just come to see how many armed men there were in the village before they attacked. But on that day, there was, unusually, a warning.

"You have until first light tomorrow," the Janjaweed leader said.

So many times since I became a refugee, people have asked me what the war in Darfur is really over. Often they confuse it with the North-South war in Sudan, which dates back to 1983 and resulted in South Sudan's independence in 2011. That war for liberation has links to our own, but the Darfur war is separate, and there are no religious differences between the two sides. In the north of Sudan, we are all Muslim. But there is an ethnic difference between many of the tribes in Darfur and the northern government in Khartoum, as tribes like mine, the Zaghawa, are African and not Arab. To some historians we were known as the "black nomads" of Darfur.

The war in Darfur began in 2003, when I was six. That's the quick version. But it's also true to say that the British laid some of the groundwork. Sudan used to be a British colony, and when it won Independence in 1956, the British set up a small Arab minority government to rule over a mostly African population, sowing the seeds for deep division in our country.

That division has been deepened further by the spoils that lie under Darfur's bare soil. For decades, the government has wanted to get its hands on the oil-rich lands across which our tribes herd our animals, caring nothing for what lies deep underneath. Khartoum has long been fed up of being the poor relation of the oil-rich Arab nations, just because a load of African nomads are standing in the way.

By 2003, the Arab government of Sudan had been oppressing Darfur's non-Arab people for decades – a situation many people compared with South African Apartheid. Tribes like mine, the Zaghawa, the Masselit, and the Fur, which give Darfur (*Home of the Fur*) its name, have always been second-class citizens, and worse, in our own country.

In 2003, the Sudan Liberation Movement and the Justice and Equality Movement began fighting the government for autonomy, launching an audacious attack on government forces in Al Fashir, the capital of north Darfur.

The government responded swiftly, with an ethnic cleansing campaign that would see families like mine wiped off the face of the earth – and Sudan's President Omar al-Bashir wanted by the International Criminal Court for genocide, war crimes, and crimes against humanity.

In many ways, of course, the rebellion was the excuse the government had been waiting for.

2004 was supposed to be a ceasefire, which the government were pretending to observe. In the meantime, the Janjaweed roamed at will, slaughtering, raping and torching every settlement they came across. The government denied that the Janjaweed acted for them when they ransacked villages and committed genocide. But everyone knew they were giving them arms and money and were even coordinating attacks.

This is the invisible genocide, which is wiping out my people, the Zaghawa, and others across Darfur. There is no record in any history book or any newspaper of what happened to our encampment, or the fact that it ever existed. In 2013, the United Nations estimated around 300,000 people met the fate I am about to describe to you. Does anyone but their families remember their names?

That's why I have to tell you this story. Because if I don't tell you about what happened to my village, who will? Of those who escaped, I am the only one I know of who is left alive.

On that day in 2004, when the Janjaweed came to our camp, my grandfather called a meeting of the whole tribe. The men gathered in the centre of the tent dressed in white and the women sat in their bright colours around the edges. They shooed us children away, but we were adept at sneaking back to listen to the adults, and the walls of tents are very thin.

"The government have asked us to leave our lands," I heard my grandfather say. "We must now discuss what we are going to do."

"We will die here!" one of the elders shouted.

"We will die martyrs!" shouted another.

"We will fight and win!" another said.

"If we let them push us away from here, they will just follow us to the next place," one of the elders said. "We have to take a stand."

"If we leave, we will become refugees or IDPs living in a camp with no dignity," another said. "I would rather die."

My grandfather listened to everyone's point of view. No-one was willing to leave our camp and to let them burn it to the ground.

"This is my proposal," he said. "We will send the children and the animals away and we will wait to see what the government will do. Prepare your children to move, and hopefully they will be back tomorrow evening when this is all over. Does everyone agree?"

Everyone agreed. Even the women, as they drew their headscarves tightly around them. The Zaghawa are a proud tribe, our men are the strongest in Sudan.

My grandfather called me to him. He looked very serious.

"Take Yusuf and the animals and go out to the grazing pastures," he said. "Look after them all until I send for you."

"But I don't want to go!" I said. I was crying. "Why do I have to go?"

"Abdul," my father said. "Listen to your grandfather. You must go."

Yusuf and I rounded up all the animals and walked very fast for half an hour, leading and herding them out into the thick forest outside the encampment. We walked quickly for a seven-year-old and a three-year-old. But we hadn't been walking very long when we heard a buzzing sound overhead. They hadn't even given us until morning. And they had sent four helicopter gunships, and tanks, instead of the Antonov.

Sudanese State Minister of Foreign Affairs Najeeb al-Kheir Abdul Wahab would later dismiss reports by the United Nations of gunship attacks across Southern Darfur in August 2004 as "baseless and untrue".

Yusuf was frightened when he heard the blades of the helicopters getting nearer. MI-24s, Khartoum's favoured machine, flying so low that I could see the Government of Sudan flag on the tail fins. We all dreaded the helicopter even more than the Antonov. The planes flew at such a height that they were barely accurate, but the helicopters were far more precise.

Moments later, we heard the sound of the helicopter beginning its barrage. Plumes of smoke began to rise on the horizon from the direction of our encampment. It sounded surreal at that distance, a popping sound more like gunfire than bombs.

Instinctively, I began to turn back towards the village, but I remembered my father's words to me, that I must protect Yusuf and the animals. For a moment I stood frozen by indecision, watching the smoke rising in the distance.

When he saw I meant to go back, Yusuf started crying.

"Don't cry, Yusuf," I said. "Don't cry. We won't go back there yet. We'll stay here and keep safe until our father and grandfather defeat the Janjaweed."

After a while, it seemed as if the barrage had stopped, so I picked up Yusuf and put him on my shoulders, and we started back towards the encampment. I thought I could hear screaming carried on the hot wind.

We had barely travelled 100 metres when a man came running towards us. I could hardly recognise him at first, so distressed and blackened was his face, but then I saw it was my father's best friend, Aboud Abdulrahman.

"Go!" Aboud was shouting. "You must go!"

He was ushering us away in the opposite direction from the encampment.

"No, Aboud!" I said. "We must go back. I can hear screaming."

"Don't go back, Abdul," he said. "Yusuf, Abdul, listen to me, don't go back. I beg you. Everything is on fire. The Janjaweed will come in behind the attack and take anything left."

"I can hear screaming," I said.

"You can't, Abdul," Aboud said. "You must come with me."

Aboud took Yusuf and me and our donkey, the only animal that had stayed with us, into the thickest part of the woods, where we stayed for what felt like hours. Yusuf was crying, and I was angry with Aboud. I had to keep calming the donkey down in case he made a noise and gave us away to passing Janjaweed.

Then we heard the sound of someone coming towards us. Aboud got ready to jump out, his knife drawn. It was Zeinab, my mum's best friend and our neighbour. Her eyes were red with crying and there was blood on her dress.

"Zeinab!" Aboud called to her.

"Oh Aboud, there's nothing left," she said. "There's no-one left alive at the camp. No-one."

I felt completely calm then. I picked Yusuf up.

"I need to go back to the camp," I said.

"Abdul, no," Aboud said. "I will go."

I pushed past Aboud. "I need to go," I told him.

I was very scared, but my mind was telling me I had to go back.

It was dusk by the time we got back to the camp. Fire was still raging through the tents and wooden sheds we had built to keep the animals safe from predators. The flickering light gave the scene an eerie glow. Apart from the cracking and splitting of the burning wood, there was no sound. No birds. No animals. No voices.

I picked my way through the flames, looking for my parents' tent, but among the blackened rags, I couldn't tell whose tent was whose. For a while I completely lost my bearings. Then I came to a pile of burning ragged clothes at the centre of the camp, from which smoke was still rising. It took me a while to realise they were human beings. Only the unbearable and unmistakable smell told me they were human remains. The clothes were badly charred, and the bodies had no faces. No hair. No scars, or tattoos. Only blackened bones.

I was trying to find my grandfather, my mother, my father, but it was like looking at broken toys. All that had survived the fire were some cooking pots and jewellery. I recognised my sister's pestle and mortar and my mother's kettle, and I knew I was looking at what was left of my family.

"We must go, Abdul!" Aboud was pulling me away. "They could still be here. The helicopter could come again. They might come back."

I saw Yusuf coming towards me and I grabbed him before he could see our family's remains. Zeinab was behind him and clapped her hand over her mouth when she saw my mother's kettle. She picked up Yusuf and started carrying him away. Aboud grabbed my hand and started pulling me.

He was a tall and strong man, with a black beard and a long robe, which was torn in places. I think he was about 30 years old. He could easily pull me along, his arm around my skinny shoulders.

"Abdul, I beg you, we must go."

We walked slowly out of the camp, and I still couldn't get my bearings, I had no idea which direction we were walking in. I only wished that the helicopter would come back and end our lives, so we didn't have to live with the pain of being without our family and remembering their burned bodies.

Then I remembered the promise I had made to my father to look after Yusuf.

"I'm coming," I said to Aboud.

We picked up our pace as we left the camp, realising we would have to get to somewhere safe by nightfall. On the way out, we passed some of the animals coming back for the evening, drawn by the smoke. Every night we would light fires to keep the lions and hyenas away, and they were used to going home when they saw them.

But there were no people in the village, just fires. Our family's spirits were already in the air, rising like smoke.

We couldn't find my beloved horses, who must have been spooked by the helicopter. So we took a donkey for the journey. Aboud said we wouldn't have food or water for more animals anyway. It would be a long walk to safety.

As we walked, I could feel the numbness I'd felt since I'd stood in the village slowly leaving me, and anger rising in its place. I couldn't rid my nose and throat of the bitter smell of burning flesh.

"Uncle," I said to Aboud after a while. "Why didn't you stay and fight?"

I was angry and I knew I was speaking rudely. I stopped walking.

Aboud said nothing.

"You are a coward!" I said.

Still Aboud said nothing.

"I'm going back to the camp," I said. "I want to die there."

"We need to keep going, Abdul," Aboud said. "Our only hope is to walk to Chad, but it's four days' walk to the border. Your grandfather knew people there. I have a relative there. We will go to the Red Cross by the border in Chad and they will help us."

"I'm not going," I said. "I will stay on my own."

"Abdul, you are too young! And there is no time to argue."

Without saying anything more, Aboud tied my hands and legs, lifted me on his back and carried me. It was the way all Zaghawa carry disobedient goats.

"I am sorry to do this to you, Abdul," Aboud said. "I have lost my own child. I am not losing another."

I hadn't thought about Aboud's family. His wife. His son. His parents. All the people we had lost. And Zeinab. What about her children? Her husband?

I was quiet then, as Aboud put me on his back and carried me like a bag.

Children in Djabal refugee camp, Chad

Chapter Three
Chad

The walk to Chad took three days through some of the most inhospitable landscape I had ever seen or have ever witnessed since. The horizon was filled with nothing but red-brown dirt and dust hovering beneath a relentlessly blue sky. Once we were far enough away from the village, Aboud put me down and untied me, and I walked next to him because I had no other people left in the world.

Little Yusuf travelled with Zeinab on the donkey. He held on to the donkey's mane and I wanted to tell my father that it had been good after all that I had taught him to ride a sheep.

On the first day, we stopped to eat whenever we saw patches of trees: mango, guava, nuts. But the lands got drier and emptier and soon there was nothing growing. We could only walk in the night when we would not be seen by the Antonov or the helicopter gunships, and the heat was more bearable.

By mid-morning each day, the sun would be pressing down on us like a heavy weight. It would be at least 40 degrees, and there was barely any shade, so we would have to stop and rest under the thin branches of a thorn tree. As we walked west, finding food and water got more and more difficult. I tried to remember the little grains that my mum would find among the grasses, and we would eat them raw, chewing them down.

Yusuf had barely spoken since we left the camp. His eyes were red, and his body hung listlessly over the donkey. Zeinab had little to say either. We were all conserving energy, and anyway, we had no words for what had happened to us.

The light played tricks on us, so that sometimes it looked as if water or people were over the horizon. In every direction we looked there was nothing but empty landscape. We felt very far from home.

Sometimes we would see the Antonov flying up above us, combing the skies, and run to hide wherever we could, dragging the donkey in after us. Our skin was scratched and red with dust. Sometimes in the far distance we could see a Land Rover, but we never knew whether it had good or bad people inside it. The dust got in our eyes and in our throats, and the wind whipped it up around us. We tried to cover our faces with our clothes, to protect ourselves from the dust and the burning sun. My eyes and throat were still raw from the smoke from the fire, and I still could not rid myself of the smell.

After two days, we met a group of armed men on the road and I was very frightened. But the men were Chadian fighters – fighting Chad's civil war, not Darfur's. They were not interested in us. Aboud asked them for directions to find the Red Cross, and they helped us onto the right road.

While our tribe, the Zaghawa, are a minority in Sudan, in Chad we are one of the dominant tribes and even the President for the last 30 years, Idriss Déby, is a Zaghawa. So we had no problem speaking the same language as the Chadian fighters we passed. One of the fighters gave us a water bottle, and another some mangos. We devoured them thirstily, the juices dripping down our faces.

Yusuf and I had been shoeless when we ran out to look after the animals and our hard feet were blistered and bleeding. Our skin was covered in dust, and our hair matted. I barely felt the thorns we slept in at night.

For days, the landscape was exactly the same: dry, bare desert with patches of thick woodland, so we didn't realise we had crossed the border. Then, suddenly, through the dust and desolation, we saw Darfuri people who were walking for firewood.

"Where are we?" Aboud asked them. "How far to the border?"

"You are safe," they told us. "You are in Chad."

I suddenly felt that I couldn't walk another step. But they stopped and gave us water and showed us the way to the camp.

Djabal refugee camp near Goz Beida was the biggest city I had ever seen, except this citadel was built out of wooden sticks, plastic bags and recycled rubbish. Home to 18,000 of the 250,000 refugees arriving in Chad to escape the unfolding genocide in Darfur, this most basic generosity is still happening despite the fact that Chad is, itself, the fifth poorest country in the world. To put this in perspective, Chad has its own bitter civil war and is on its knees because of drought and ethnic and tribal conflicts. Despite being the same size as Peru or South Africa, it is a country with only one paved road.

We didn't know it, but we had just walked into the biggest aid operation anywhere in the world at that time. In 2004, at the height of the Darfur terror campaign, 13,000 aid workers and over 100 relief organisations were working across the region inside Chad and Darfur itself. In Djabal, some of the structures were proper tents with the names of aid agencies printed on them in large, bright letters. But most people were living in tents made out of long sticks taken from the trees, rubbish bags and any bits of clothing or blankets they could find.

When we arrived, we were very weak, and someone took us to find the white people in charge of the camp. They were the very first white people I had ever seen. I was too tired to stare at these pale ghosts, caught by the sun, as much as I would have liked to. They gave us clean water to drink and some fufu in a bowl. I don't remember thinking anything about them, except for remembering my grandfather's words about the white men with green eyes and cars. All I could think about was my parents, my sisters and my grandfather's bodies burned in the village, and how tired I was.

We were led to the shade of a feeding centre and were fed a kind of juice from orange plastic cups, and then Yusuf and I were given pouches of "plumpy nut", a food supplement you swallow straight from the packet. It just tastes of sugar and salt, but I could feel my body craving it, pulling it down into my stomach. I immediately felt sick and had to lie down in the shade. Yusuf had already fallen asleep against the side of the tent, the Plumpy nut packet in his slackened hand.

Inside the tent, the weak cries of babies and small children rose and fell like the camp inhaling and exhaling. Outside, I could see camp life – a life we would soon know well – going on around the centre. Girls in worn-out dresses faded by the sun walked by with firewood piled on their heads, and children younger than Yusuf passed us carrying buckets of water the same way. The boys' clothing was often ripped or threadbare too, and their faces streamed with eye infections and the beaded sweat of malarial fevers. Women with downcast eyes passed with heavy white jerry cans, still holding the strong, tall posture for which Darfuris are famed.

I spoke to a boy lying next to me on the tarpaulin. He replied in Zaghawa, saying he was sick with some sort of dysentery, which was why he was drinking the plumpy nut.

"I'm Mohamed," he said. "How old are you?"

"Seven," I said.

"I'm eight," he said, happy to be the older boy.

"How is it here?" I said. The world was still spinning around my head and I felt like I might vomit.

"You are safer than Darfur, but it is really a prison," Mohamed said. "Is your family dead?"

"Yes," I said. "Apart from Yusuf, my little brother."

"You are lucky," Mohamed said.

I asked how long he had been here.

"A year, I think," he said. "I don't know any more."

After some food and rest, we were sent to the centre for processing. We were registered with a blue biro in a big red book by a man in important-looking black wellington boots. He was from the Masalit tribe, but wearing a T-shirt like the white people wore, with a Red Cross on it, and had an air of being very pleased with himself.

The official spoke to us in French first. France used to be the colonial power in Chad, like Britain was in Sudan. We said we didn't speak any French, so he spoke to us in Arabic. Like the Zaghawa, the Masalit exist on both sides of the Chadian border, and he seemed very at home.

The official in wellingtons said we would have to be interviewed about our journey and the reasons we had left our encampment, to find out if we were economic migrants looking for work, refugees from Darfur, or internally displaced from inside Chad. But he added that he was writing down that he knew we were Zaghawa. Many people, he said, were arriving from the same series of government and Janjaweed raids across South Darfur.

We were talking to him when the familiar sound of an approaching aeroplane buzzed through the air, and Yusuf and I ran for cover. As we cowered behind a table at the edge of the tent, we were aware of people laughing.

"Those are the kawagas' planes, the white people!" the official said. "They won't hurt you. They come in from N'Djamena with the food supplies and medicines."

He narrowed his eyes. "You must still look out for the Antonov, because they fly over, looking for rebels and spying on us, but they are not allowed to bomb here. We are in Chad, not Sudan. They can't bomb another country."

Aboud went to find the elders to tell them the sad news of our camp and to find out what they knew of any other survivors. He was looking for my grandfather's friend, but no-one knew him.

In the crowded camp, so many men were missing that committees of women elders – who always met in Darfur but were usually below the male committees of elders – were now making many important decisions. Even so, the main decisions were made by Sheikhs, elders who had the backing of rebel leaders. The songs in the camp – even those sung by children – were odes to the Sudan Liberation Army leader Abdul Wahid. If anything, we were now even more embroiled in a war we wanted nothing to do with.

We were assigned to an area of the camp that contained Zaghawa people from South Darfur. Many of our neighbours were newly arrived too, ethnically cleansed in the same offensive that had destroyed our encampment, and there was an air of chaos and arrival.

Aboud and Zeinab were not husband and wife, but we were all assigned a space to shelter together as a family. We were given plastic sheeting, a jerry can, soap, and a pot for cooking. Aboud and Zeinab made a shelter out of the sheeting to keep the sun from blazing down on us, the wind from blowing dust in our eyes, and in case of rain.

The landscape in Chad looked as if it hadn't had any rain in centuries. It is a land so far from the sea, and its desert climate means it is often known as The Dead Heart of Africa.

Even so, our neighbours told us the rains would soon be coming. They said June to September was a new kind of hell.

"You think it is bad now," an older lady told us. "Wait until the rains have turned this camp to filthy mud and disease goes around, cholera and diarrhoea. Then you will wish you had died in Darfur."

The shelter had separate compartments. I slept in one with Aboud, and Yusuf slept in the other with Zeinab. Of course, in truth, I never really slept at all, but just kept staring into the blackness night after night, and I suspect it was the same for the others. I would hear them tossing and turning and crying out in the night, and sometimes

Aboud or Zeinab would get up and kneel in the entrance to the tent, staring out into the sky.

All night we would hear the shooting out in the bush, the rat-a-tat of gunfire and then gunfire returned in armed skirmishes, the screams of women, and the howls of wild animals. Even the stars were different in Chad and didn't seem to burn as brightly as in Darfur.

Aboud was thin after all the days of walking, but he said he was strong, and would soon be well again. He said he would get a job in the camp and look after us. Zeinab was the same age as my mother, about 25. She told Yusuf and me she was going to look after us just like my mum. She kept her promise. Under the most difficult circumstances, she tried to make the best of the meagre camp rations, washing and mending our clothes when there was water or thread, and trying to keep our shelter swept of the thick dust. Under her breath I would catch her singing the same songs my mother sang and I remembered the closeness of their friendship.

Aboud got a job selling tea from a flask in the village near to the camp, where lots of refugees worked unofficially. He saved up to buy a radio so that we could hear news of the war in Sudan and when we might be able to go home to Darfur. Apart from the radio, by now we had a couple of blankets to sleep on, a couple of cooking pots, a grill to put over the fireplace, and the plastic jerry can for water. We had no mosquito nets, and the sticks had gaps that let the cold night air in.

We were trapped in the camp because when refugees left it to collect firewood, they were regularly attacked by armed militias or wild animals. Zeinab told us never ever to go outside the camp. But she had to go for water and firewood. Sometimes she would come back distressed and not speak to us. We heard the rumours that women were regularly attacked.

Every day, new arrivals from Darfur would bring news of different villages under attack, or sometimes welcome news of relatives or friends who had survived or were living in such-and-such refugee camp or IDP camp. Rebel fighters came too, to visit their families, rest and resupply. They were treated as heroes, sipping tea in the burning sunshine, their eyes behind black sunglasses so no-one could see what they had seen.

The days stretched into weeks, and we understood the painful monotony of living in a refugee camp. We woke up and prayed, we fetched water from the stand-pipe, we collected wood from the thorn forest, we lit small cooking fires, we ate the same rations, we slept on the same hard floor, and we were still frightened when the planes came overhead.

We were vaccinated and questioned and sent for registration. We buried our neighbours when they died in the camp from disease. Sometimes I walked the length of the camp to go to the school, but it was always so full by the time I got there that you couldn't even see into the tent.

We were always hungry and always thirsty. The effects of malnutrition were visible everywhere we went, in the reddish tint of our thin black curls, the stunting of our height, and our hard, swollen stomachs. Children of five years of age looked like toddlers, and babies' bones jutted through their papery skin.

Our family was only allowed five litres of water per person, where the United Nations recommendation was 15 litres. Eventually we were given some mosquito nets, but one hungry day Aboud sold them for food.

Inside the camps, people tried to make a home for themselves. There were little barber's shops set up with just a bucket, a razor and a mirror tied to a stick. There were ladies who would make clothes, sometimes re-stitching the same cloth over and over, and men who made hooch and traded in rare dusty cans of fizzy drinks. Little markets would suddenly be set up on pieces of cloth for those who had any money. An impromptu butcher's would appear in an alleyway, a goat hacked into strips left swinging in the sun to dry, suspended from wooden sticks. Entrepreneurial young men went from tent to tent offering solar-powered charging for anyone who'd come from a city and was lucky enough to have a mobile phone.

Yusuf and I would waste precious drops of water to make dust into mud and sculpt little statues of giraffe and buffalo and horses. If we boys found a little piece of barbed wire, we would sculpt it into an aeroplane or make a walkie-talkie like the kawagas, the white people, carried. We would play endless games with these priceless toys.

There would be outbreaks of singing when the women would dance and perform joyful songs that all Zaghawa know. People got married and had babies, and lost babies. All of human life was in the refugee camp, and yet it wasn't a life. As the boy told me the day we arrived in Djabal, it was really a prison.

To any Darfuri, eastern Chad is a living hell. It is a barren, boiling desert, a million miles from the oases we were always able to visit, the places of verdant vegetation, oranges and plentiful water. Chad is as inhospitable as Planet Earth gets. The relentless sun, constant dust and lack of shade lead to a kind of madness. There is a skull in the museum of N'Djamena, the capital, that is seven million years old, and many people say Chad is where the first human beings came from. It is not hard to imagine our ancestors stretching back into that desert where it feels like time has long ago stopped.

Staying in the camp was its own kind of unending poverty and misery. We were hungry every day, and there was never enough water. Our place in the camp was a long way from the school, and it wasn't safe for us to travel. Our stick-and-tarpaulin homes provided little shelter from the dry heat, the cold winds or the diseases that swept through the camp. In every patch of shade lay someone with malaria, diarrhoea, sickness, typhoid, HIV, or someone nursing green infected wounds or swollen snake bites. Sometimes cholera camps had to be set up out in the bush to keep the infected separate from the main refugee body. We would pass the neat white lines of the hospital tents travelling with Zeinab to fetch firewood or water and say a prayer for the people as we passed.

No-one wanted to stay, but Djabal was a curious kind of imprisonment. It wasn't illegal to travel out of the camps into Chad, but there was nowhere to go. The walls of this prison were invisible – the burning heat, distant gunfire, lack of water, and the impossibility of getting to anywhere else that could sustain human life. Every indigenous village was suffering its own battles with the parched, war-torn landscape. Every Chadian family faced its own battle for survival.

To the west was N'Djamena – 750 kilometres away, across land controlled by warring factions, troops, militias and warrior tribes. To the east was Darfur and certain death. So instead, many Darfuri refugees looked north to Libya. It would mean a dangerous journey of more than a thousand miles across the Sahara desert, in the hands of traffickers. And the very best outcome at the other end was to find hard labour as an illegal migrant in a country run by a despot, Colonel Gaddafi. But it was better than receiving handouts in a refugee camp for decade upon decade. And better than waiting to die from cholera with only a plastic jerry can to your name.

Sometime in 2007, when we had been in the camp for almost three whole years, people in the camp started saying the war in Darfur was over and it was safe to go home, but Aboud only trusted the reports on his radio.

"It's not safe to go back," he said. "They killed our whole families, they killed our animals, if we go back, they will kill us."

Zeinab said she dreamed of going back. We all dreamed of going back and getting out of this desert hell.

"There is no-one there for us," Aboud said. "All our family and all our friends are dead. And it is not safe. It is a trap."

Rumours swept the camp that we would all be returned to Darfur within weeks, because the Chadian authorities – who, after all, were too poor to sustain us – said the war was over. The rebels coming from Darfur brought different news. The scorched-earth policy continued. Meanwhile, entire parts of our homeland were now empty of settlements, animals and human beings.

Aboud just listened to the radio and shook his head.

One black night, when I was about ten and Yusuf was about six, Yusuf shook me awake. I was confused to find that Aboud wasn't lying next to me.

"He's next door talking to Zeinab," Yusuf said.

Yusuf was crying. For the last few days he had been very ill with malaria, sweating and feverish, and had been in the hospital tent. Tonight, he had been allowed back to stay with us, but I felt his forehead and it was burning.

"Aboud and Zeinab thought I was asleep, but I wasn't," he said. "Abdul, Aboud is going to take you away, to Libya," he said. "I heard him say it. He said, 'I will take Abdulkareem and we will send for you when we find somewhere to live, and have work, and have the money to send to you to travel.' He actually swore on the Koran he will come back."

I felt my blood go cold. Yusuf couldn't stop crying.

"We have to go back to Darfur," Yusuf said. "We have to go now. Mum and dad are sleeping, and we have to be there when they wake up." He was delirious with fever. "I want mum and dad!" he said.

Yusuf was only three years old when we left Darfur. He was only six now. I realised he didn't understand our mum and dad were never going to wake up. I couldn't bear to tell him the truth, that they were dead.

"It's just a dream, Yusuf," I said, putting my arm round him. "You are sick, and you need to sleep. Aboud would never separate us."

I couldn't think about it because my heart was hurting so much.

We left for Libya the next day, Aboud and me. Aboud said Yusuf was not well enough to travel and that it would be even more dangerous for Zeinab to travel with us into Libya than it was for her to remain in the camp.

"Yusuf is only six years old, Abdul, and our journey is not safe," Aboud said. "We will go first. We will find work, we will work hard, and then we will send for them when we have a place to live and an income. If the Chadian government try to close the camp and send our people back to Darfur, then Zeinab already has a plan to move further into Chad where your grandfather has friends. She will wait there until we can send for her."

I felt a physical pain at the thought of leaving Yusuf, my little brother and the last living member of my family, but Aboud persuaded me we would see him soon. We would lead the way and come back for him. I thought of being in the dusty camp for year after year, or in the promised land of Libya, a place with seas and oases, and cities of plenty. A place we could find work and make a life for ourselves. I had nothing to lose except my brother.

In all my dreams I see Yusuf's face when we left. His eyes were red with illness and he was crying and trying to run after us.

"We will send for you soon, Yusuf," I told him. "This is the best thing to do. You have to let us go, and then we will send for you."

"Please, Abdul." Over and over again, I see him. "Please, Abdul."

Refugees at Djabal refugee camp, Chad

Chapter Four
Libya

I was seven years old when I left Darfur for Chad, and 10 years old when I left Chad to go to Libya. Libya was the place everyone in the refugee camp talked of going to, as if it were a kind of promised land. In 2007, its leader Colonel Gaddafi was attempting to improve his international reputation and even won a seat for Libya on the UN Security Council. The country appeared to be becoming more stable. In truth, it was a brutal dictatorship, known for repeated human rights violations.

All that mattered to us was that Libya was booming with oil wealth and construction projects, and it was possible for illegal migrants to find underground work in building roads, houses and engineering ventures. We could sell our hard labour to wealthy Libyans. We had no intention of trying to get to Europe, a place I had never even heard of. Just to get to somewhere we could earn money and live like human beings.

The border between Chad and Libya, like the border between Darfur and Chad, didn't really exist. It was too vast to be policed except along a very few paths. Chad was full of training camps for Libyan rebels who moved across the border at will. At some points one country blurred into the other – no man's lands that had belonged to one country or another at different times, depending on who had drawn the borders.

That morning in 2007, Aboud and I set off from Djabal Refugee Camp at daybreak. We had nothing to take with us apart from a water carrier, a small amount of food and a blanket. As we walked, Yusuf's cries were still ringing in my ears.

We walked a long way through the scrubland towards Goz Beida. Eventually, we came upon a truck that gave us a lift in the direction we were travelling. By nightfall, we had reached the outskirts of the town of Abéché, a military and aid agency hub and a former stronghold of the Arabic slave trade route.

The roads were unpaved, yet as busy as any highway, with armed aid convoys coming in and out of the city. Reassuringly, these giant lorries weighed down with soldiers and weapons or sacks of grain had to negotiate the paths of donkeys piled high with produce and jerry cans, or dragging carts behind them, and the tarmac soon ran out into dust. The air was alive with beeping horns, slammed brakes, shouts and the late call to prayer from the two minarets dominating the skyline.

In the sky above, the last charter flights of the day were coming in to land on Abéché airstrip, bringing aid and oil workers to the region.

At the allotted point, groups of men sat on their heels in the dust carrying a few belongings tied up in cloth. Others were sharing the thin shelter of a thorn tree. I only saw two women among the group, their heads and faces covered, and their eyes cast into shade. Abéché is the hottest city in Chad and one of the hottest cities on earth, and even at this late hour, the heat felt like a punch, reflected by the hard roads.

After a while, a lorry arrived, and people began clamouring to get on. By the time Aboud and I jumped aboard, there were so many people packed onto the back of it that it was hard to breathe. The roof was covered by a big tarpaulin, and very hot inside. Even so, the driver jumped down and pulled it tightly over the frame, locking it into place and crushing the rest of the air out of the vehicle. I could see a pistol tucked into his belt.

Aboud told me we were being smuggled into Libya illegally because we didn't have any papers. He had to pay the people traffickers to take us there.

"The driver has already paid all the people at the border," he said. "Don't worry, Abdul. It won't be a very comfortable journey, but we will soon be in Libya."

I was still upset about leaving Yusuf, especially when he was so ill with malaria. I had no understanding of how far we were going. Aboud told me not to worry. "I will find work in Libya," he said. "We'll make a home, and you will go to school, and we will send for Zeinab and Yusuf."

He smiled at me. "You were your grandfather's favourite grandson," he said, "and you are strong and brave like him. I will protect you, like I once protected him."

Migration patterns have changed across Chad in the years since I made my journey, but it has been at the centre of many human trafficking routes since the slave trade. The stories we hear of migrants often focus on sea crossings, but the journey across the Sahara is one of the most dangerous of all, perhaps because its victims are invisible. Who knows how many trafficked people have been left to die in the desert, unseen by any agency and unrecorded by any pen or camera.

The people on our lorry would have had many motives: trade, work, escaping death or hunger, going to fight in Libya, or dreaming of Europe's shores. We all shared one motivation: to make a better, safer life.

I have no way of knowing the route we took from Abéché, but the most common route in 2007 for Darfuri migrants coming from the camps was via the Saharan city of Faya in Chad, where temperatures regularly reach 49 degrees. Faya had been under Libyan occupation until 1987, adding to the sense of blurred borders. From there, in the 2000s, most routes went up to Libya's migrant-smuggling capital of Kufra, in the south-east of the country.

Passengers travelled – and travel still – on large trucks used to bring livestock from Libya to Chad, returning with goods from Chad that hide their human cargo. From time to time, our truck stopped to let armed convoys pass, off to fight on one front or another. Our driver, like many across these routes, was Zaghawa. In Chad, unlike Sudan, it was easy for Zaghawa men to move around. The Chadian Army largely left us alone because of the Zaghawa President.

I don't know how many days we travelled in that packed truck or when we crossed the border into Libya. We were hungry, thirsty and exhausted again, and we were travelling even further from our home, in the wrong direction. But going home meant certain death, and Chad was a dusty hell.

Each night we would be let out to stretch our legs, urinate, and the driver would try to extort money out of some of his passengers at gunpoint or bother the women. These breaks were frightening, yet the feel of air – even the still air of the desert – against my cheek felt wonderful, even as my muscles struggled to unfurl themselves from the cramped position they had held for many hours. Freed for a few moments, the passengers would share what little water and food we had, and joke a little with each other, trying to share what was left of us as human beings. I often wondered about the other people's stories. What wars were they escaping? What famines? What personal strife? Or were they just looking for a new life?

Up above, the stars in that desert were the most extraordinary I had ever seen – tiny points of light caught up in great swirls and patterns, occasionally framing the silhouettes of camels, which were the only living things to break the horizon. Below my feet was a kind of sand I had never stood on or experienced. It wasn't the firm, dry, rocky dirt I had grown up on, but soft, so that your feet sank into it, creating vast dunes up and down which our vehicle climbed. In the brief moments we were able to glimpse it, it spread out like a sea, wave after sugary wave.

I had no idea what Libya would be like. Was it a desert, or full of cities? Would it have lush vegetation or dry riverbeds? Most of the journey I spent looking into the blackness of the packed lorry, listening to the straining engine and the men shouting Arabic stories to each other, dreaming of a cool cup of water for my parched mouth, or some biscuits for the hard knot in my stomach.

Our lorry came through back roads into Libya. Someone would have been paid not to see it pass into the country. Or given that 90 per cent of Libya, a country 85 times the size of Wales, is uninhabited, and that 80 per cent of Libyans live up on the north coast, there may have been no-one to see us. Our first indication that we were in a new country was hearing people speak Arabic in a new dialect, and feeling the vehicle fly along new, good roads as we continued on through the desert.

The lorry abandoned us as quickly as it had picked us up, in barren scrubland outside Kufra. We were told to walk into town, where we could pick up work. We were all hungry, thirsty and exhausted. Some of the men were staggering after being trapped on the vehicle for so many days. We agreed to split up and move under cover of darkness. We were illegal migrants now, in a country where we spoke the wrong dialect and no longer had connections with the military.

Kufra has long been a border town. Its name comes from *Kafir*, "non-Arab", literally "infidel". It is an oasis inside a basin surrounded by the Sahara on all sides. Aboud had an address for a man in Kufra who it was said could organise work on a building site in return for food and shelter. It was all we had to pin our hopes on – some words written on a piece of paper.

It felt good to be in a normal town instead of a refugee camp. We passed markets with women selling goods on wooden tables, a camel-trading marketplace, and pens full of livestock. Aboud had a few small coins in his pocket, Chadian money, which he exchanged for watermelon, which we swallowed thirstily. We passed little kiosks with music playing, and shops with bright fabric hung from the walls. Trucks thundered through the narrow streets, scattering stall holders and ladies chatting in the shade. Here, as everywhere, soldiers from various factions, and in various pieces of camouflage wear, sat around drinking tea or smoking at cafes.

Aboud and I found the address on the piece of paper, a flat-roofed house in a town of domes and minarets. A man there gave us some water to drink, and drove us to a building site on the outskirts of the town. Sudanese and Chadian migrants were crammed into a dilapidated hostel there, sleeping 20 to a room. They welcomed us, asking us for news of Darfur and Djabal and Abéché.

"How old is the boy?" the gangmaster asked.

Aboud shot me a look before I could reply that I was 10 years old.

"He is 13," he said.

We worked on the building site from dawn until long after nightfall, usually from 6am until 10pm, making bricks and cement, and dragging carts of rocks and carrying water. For this effort we were allowed to sleep on mattresses on the floor of the hostel and fed one bowl of food a day, usually some kind of fufu with a bit of stew. There were other children there, some even younger than me. We were given the work of breaking rocks and sorting stones into different sizes. The stones and dust got into our eyes, and there was very little shade.

When we finished our shift, Aboud would wait at the roadside to pick up other building work. I would wait for him anxiously at the hostel, 10 years old and far from home.

"We won't be here long, Abdul," Aboud told me. "Just until we get some money together to get us to Ajdabiya."

Aboud had friends from Djabal who had already made it to Ajdabiya. They said there was plenty of work there, and landlords that accepted Darfuri migrants.

We were lucky in Kufra. There were so many stories of illegal migrants being rounded up by the police and beaten, or robbed at gunpoint by militias. Others were simply abducted, taken into the desert and forced to work for free as slaves.

For four months, we lived in squalid conditions and lived the life of the outdoor sweatshop. But we escaped with our lives, our freedom and enough money for the journey north.

Chapter Five
Ajdabiya

Four months after arriving in Libya, we set off from Kufra into the dry heat of the interior for the promised land of Ajdabiya in northern Libya. Aboud had bought our passage on another hot, dark truck travelling through the desert, another classic route for migrants trying to make it to the coast. This time our truck was filled with migrants from all kinds of countries: Sudan, Ethiopia, Chad, Somalia. Women and children were on board too. Some were heading for ports like Benghazi or Tripoli in the hope of crossing dangerous seas to Europe. Others, like us, just wanted to find work in Ajdabiya where everyone had heard migrants could earn good money with no questions asked.

The driver was Libyan, a hard-faced man who liked to gesture with his assault rifle. Once we were packed in, the cargo was packed behind us, boxes of fruit and vegetables. Again, we were hungry and thirsty, but after a month breaking rocks in 40-degree heat in Kufra, at least we could rest our bodies in the lorry as it rocked and swayed and bumped along the roads.

Again, we were taken out at night to stretch our legs and sometimes given water and a few biscuits. Then we were jammed back into the boiling lorry to sweat again under the tarpaulin. Some of the women would sing to comfort their crying children and I would feel the presence of my mother looking after me during the journey.

After three days, we arrived through a giant green gate into an endless, noisy traffic jam of trucks and cars. Brick houses formed orderly lines along dusty streets, interspersed with tented encampments. Beyond them, tall, modern buildings made of concrete, traditional domed structures, and turreted minarets scraped the sky. Ajdabiya was an oil town at a strategically important crossroads between Tripoli and Benghazi and routes south towards oases in the desert.

We stood in its largest square and marvelled at the city and the blue cloudless skies above.

When we arrived in 2007, Ajdabiya was a bustling oil town with plenty of work. It had a big concrete hospital, municipal headquarters, police stations and schools. Its population was expanding, with Libyan nomads moving in from the desert and needing homes. Houses and offices needed building all over the city and cheap migrant labour was unofficially welcomed.

Within four years, it would be at the heart of the 2011 Libyan uprising, a rebel stronghold that would feel the full force of Colonel Gaddafi's revenge, then become a ghost town. In the near future, the large square we stood in would be renamed Tim Hetherington Square after the British war photographer killed by a shrapnel wound in Misrata. For a long time, the square's name would just be marked on a simple white flag torn from a hospital sheet.

We arrived in the morning at a four-storey apartment block in 7 October district that belonged to a Libyan man called Ibrahim Issa. There was a Darfuri family living there who Aboud knew. They greeted us warmly and gave us tea and breakfast.

It was the first time I had ever been in an apartment – a house on top of another house. The building might have been run down by Libyan standards, but to us it looked like paradise. They had running water, electricity, brick walls, a tiled bathroom. It was very crowded. 10 people lived there already and now we were two more, but they still welcomed us. At times more than 20 people lived in the two-bedroom apartment.

There were five other children who lived there, and they quickly became my friends. A boy, Abdul Bari, and two girls, who were around my age. Then there were two little children called Fatima and Abdul Sadik. The children already spoke the Libyan dialect, which helped me to learn it too.

None of us children could go to school because we were all illegal immigrants. This was true of many of our neighbours in this district of Ajdabiya, which was often subject to police and army raids to round up illegals. The other children showed me where to hide if soldiers came, and how never to answer the door if there were no adults around. Usually the soldiers were paid off by the Libyans who employed illegal immigrants.

The men from the family went to work at various different places – tiling companies, building sites, gardening jobs and labouring. The women looked after Ibrahim Issa's large house, cooking and cleaning and doing whatever domestic chores needed doing. I helped the mothers with the housework – cleaning the house, helping in the kitchen, helping carry the shopping. It was domestic servitude, but I didn't mind doing it. I was now 10 years old and happy to earn my keep.

Of all the jobs, I particularly enjoyed cooking, pounding the cassava for fufu, chopping endless mountains of chillis and onions, and simmering stews on the stovetop. As well as the Darfuri dishes I had watched my mother and sister cooking, I learned to cook Libyan food, with its influences of Italian, Mediterranean, North African and Berber foods. It was where I first ate pasta, and where I loved to stuff dates, figs, olives and dried apricots into my mouth.

As well as Libyan Arabic, I learned Italian, which Ibrahim Issa and his friends spoke. I learned that where Britain had once ruled over Sudan and Chad had been conquered by France, Italy had taken Libya when the European powers shared out our continent.

When there was no work, I played with the other children in the street. We didn't have any toys, but we invented many different games that usually involved chasing each other and running around. Sometimes we would get hold of a ball and play catch or kick the ball. Some of the children liked to play war games, but I always refused. I had seen an army come and kill my parents and burn down my village. I would never, ever play at war.

Aboud worked with lots of other Sudanese, gardening, building, doing any jobs he could find to get money to put food on the table. I kept hoping it was time to send for Yusuf and Zeinab, but it was never the right time.

After a few months, Aboud got a job as a driver in Benghazi for a Libyan man. He said it wasn't safe for me to go with him, so I stayed in Ajdabiya. On his day off, every Friday, Aboud would travel to see me, a 100-kilometre journey each way, and three hours on the fast bus. He was well paid in Benghazi and brought back money for the family to look after me and to help with bills at the house.

Life in Libya wasn't really paradise, but it was better than the camp and better than perishing in the desert. We didn't have much – our accommodation was cramped, and we had to keep an eye out for the police – but we were safe from bombs, we had enough food to eat and water to drink, and we had clothes on our backs. We lived like a family and laughed together.

Sometimes I used to walk all the way to the turquoise sea near Brega, and walk along the beach, looking out into the Mediterranean. It was a long way to the next landfall – Italy or Greece – and all I could see was seawater, or more of the curved Libyan coastline. I never met anyone else there, only seabirds.

I had been in Libya for almost two years, and had recently celebrated my 12th birthday with my new Darfuri family, when I was sent on a housekeeping errand to the market. A jeep stopped suddenly in front of me, jolting me out of a daydream. Suddenly, I realised there were police cars and army vehicles stopping all over the streets.

Two soldiers got out of the vehicle and grabbed me by the arms. My heart was pounding in my chest.

I protested I had done nothing wrong, but they were in no mood to listen.

"Where are your papers?" one of the soldiers asked.

He seemed to be the officer in charge. I spoke in my best Libyan accent.

"They are at home."

"I don't believe you," the officer said. "You are an illegal immigrant. You will go to jail and then you will be deported to whatever African country you came from. Or you can fight for Colonel Gaddafi. Which do you choose?"

"I won't fight," I said. "My parents were killed by war and I don't want to kill anyone. I will never, ever fight in anyone's army."

"All the Africans are fighting for Colonel Gadaffi now," the officer said. "You will be conscripted or go back to your country and rot."

"I am only 12 years old," I said. "I am too young for the army."

"12 years old is plenty old enough to fight," the officer said.

"I won't fight," I said.

The officer sucked his teeth and gestured to the other soldier.

"Take him to the camp for illegal immigrants."

The officers threw me in a truck with about 30 other people, all clearly frightened. There were some other children my age too. We didn't know where we were going. We were all migrants from different countries. One man was from Niger, another from Central African Republic. Some of the children were crying. We were given no food, only water, and we were in the lorry for a long time.

When we started off, I began to suspect we were going back to be dumped in Chad. All our long journey would have been for nothing. I would die in the desert because I wouldn't even be able to find my way back to Abéché and I had no paperwork even to say I was from Darfur.

It was the first time since I had been a child of seven years old that I was travelling without Aboud, the man who had taken care of me out of love for my father. When

I didn't come back with the shopping, I knew my Libyan Darfuri family would comb the streets for me. Eventually they would realise I had been taken and send a message to Aboud. But what could any of them do? How would anyone ever find me in the back of this army truck hurtling through the dark, travelling to an unknown destination?

For the first time, in a very long time, I allowed myself to cry. Unlike the other children in the army truck, there was no-one to put their arm round me and tell me it would be okay. My parents and my sisters were dead. My brother was hundreds of miles away in a refugee camp. Aboud was in Benghazi. I was somewhere in the vast, scalding expanse of Libya, completely and utterly alone.

Chapter Six
Sirte

The truck kept on rolling for 100 miles along the coast road, before stopping at the locked gates of a prison complex. Night had fallen again, and when soldiers opened the truck to look at us, we were temporarily blinded by security lights. The truck drove inside the complex and we were all ordered down and told to line up. The soldiers took everything – watches, shoes, money, anything we had on us.

We had arrived at a series of low buildings surrounding a central courtyard, themselves surrounded by barbed wire and lit by bright lights. From dark windows, we were aware of hundreds of faces staring out. A man was beaten for looking the guard in the eye.

The army camp, in a dusty outpost near Sirte, was run by Colonel Gaddafi's son Khamis, the feared military leader who commanded the elite 32nd brigade of the

Libyan Army. He never spoke to us directly, but we would see him at a distance, striding around the camp in his combat fatigues, or in the windows of an armoured car. Attached to the camp was a prison full of African migrants who had refused to fight or otherwise fallen foul of the Gaddafi regime, or just been in the wrong place at the wrong time.

By 2009 when I arrived there, it was a living hell run by army officers and people smugglers. Migrants died here without ever making it to the Mediterranean to die in the sea. Like all these detention centres across Libya, the prison in Sirte was part of a corrupt conveyor belt, where detainees bought their way out only to be returned and re-arrested weeks or months later. Detainees disappeared overnight and reappeared again, depending on who they had or hadn't paid. Meanwhile, the conditions inside were squalid and violent.

When I arrived at the prison, I was thrown into a cell that was little more than a big hole. It was packed with around 30 men and boys, and I never saw the people I was in the lorry with again. The cells were cramped and filthy, and already too full of people. I was one of the youngest there, but there were two boys who were even younger than me. We came from different African countries riven by conflict, drought and famine: Sudan, Chad, Niger, Central African Republic, and even as far away as Somalia.

For the first few days I wasn't mistreated, but conditions were very harsh. Food was brought to the cell once a day or sometimes once every two days. Sometimes we were served a small breakfast of lentils and beans in the morning, or a fist-sized amount of plain pasta in the evening, sometimes with cheese, or sometimes just rice. Drinking water came from a tap in the cell.

There were no toilets in the cell, and we had to ask if we wanted to go, and to be brought out of the cell. Every few days we were taken to shower. Someone had a ball we would pass between each other inside the cell.

Through the wall we could hear the sound of the beatings, and the screaming of men being tortured. Inmates would whisper about the worse fate of the women and girls. Men would come back to the cell with burst lips and black eyes, and women would come back in silence, covering their faces with their headscarves.

The hours turned into days, and then a week passed, and then two. I was very hungry all the time, and the cell was cramped and filthy. Many of the people in the cells were sick or injured, and we barely spoke. There was a bunch of rolled-up rags that I and the two other boys would silently roll between each other like a ball to take up the time.

Like everyone in the cell, I lived in constant fear of being singled out by the guards. I hated being taken to the toilet, as I would be on my own with them. I knew they would come for me eventually. No-one escaped their attention forever.

One day, the guards came and called my name. I was immediately frightened.

"Abdul, you have a visitor."

They led me to the visitors' room and there was Aboud. I couldn't believe my eyes. To see him there was the most wonderful thing. He had found me – and he had risked his own life and safety to visit me. As an African migrant, they could have arrested him then and there and thrown him into jail with me.

Aboud had brought his new employer with him, a Libyan, who was able to vouch for him. The employer was trying to help me, but the guards said there was no way I would be released.

Aboud had brought me some food and drinks, and he gave me some money so I could buy extra food in prison. In the end, Aboud had to make the long journey back to Benghazi with his employer but he said he would come back whenever he could, and they would try to free me.

At least from that day onwards in the prison I knew I wasn't completely alone. Aboud knew where I was. I felt a little bit less hopeless, even though I knew I still could be returned to Sudan at any time, and the conditions were very bad at the prison even with a little bit of extra money.

Then, one day, the guards came for me again. This time there was no sign of Aboud. I was taken into an interview room. Four guards came with me. They were carrying wooden bats and iron coshes, as they always did.

"You need to make a choice, Abdul," one of the guards said. "Think carefully before you answer."

I nodded. The men were all standing very close to me.

"You need to join the army. Brother Leader needs fighters. Do you choose to join or be thrown back to Sudan?"

"If I go back to Darfur I will die," I said.

"Then join the army," they said. "You will get money and weapons. You will be safe."

"I can't fight," I told them. "I will never fight because of what happened to my family."

The men looked at each other.

They began to beat me with the bats and coshes. The blows rained down on me, and I couldn't protect my head. I was bleeding very badly from my left knee.

"Which do you choose, Abdul?"

I was very tired, and my head hurt, but I said I couldn't choose to go home and I couldn't choose to fight.

After that, I was beaten every day. They would drag me out of the cell and beat me with the bats and coshes. They snapped my finger. I have never been able to straighten it ever since. It remains locked in the position they left it in.

It seemed as if everyone was getting beatings at that time. We were all injured, tired and very thin. I started getting sick, but they still didn't stop. Even back in the cell, I couldn't stand up, I just stayed on the floor.

Then one day, they brought me into the room, and they sat me in a chair. I didn't understand at first what they were doing. They had electricity cables, and they attached them to my ear and my back. Then they put the other ends into a bucket of water. They electrocuted me. I still have the burn marks on my body. These are the things I carry with me. My tribal markings, and the burn marks where they tortured me.

That time, when they beat me, the metal bar hit my head and I passed out.

I woke up in hospital with no idea how much time had gone by since I had passed out. My body was still in shock and pain from the electrocution, and my finger was hurting badly. Most of all, my head was throbbing where the metal bar had hit me. I was blinded by my headache and overcome with nausea. My mouth tasted of blood.

That was the first time I had been in a bed in many months, and the mattress felt very soft. There was a strange man sitting next to my bed. A doctor dressed in a blue surgical uniform, with a stethoscope around his neck. He was a very tall and overweight Western man, with blue eyes and blonde hair. He looked enormous to me after the thin shadows I shared a cell with.

He spoke to me in Arabic with a strange accent. I wish I could remember his name.

"What's your name?" the doctor said.

I spoke with difficulty through the headache and because my mouth was swollen.

"Abdul."

He asked me how old I was.

"I'm 12 years old," I told him.

"Are you Libyan?"

"I'm Sudanese," I said. "I come from Darfur."

After two years in Libya, I had become fluent in the local dialect, and people often mistook me now for a Libyan.

"You are the same age as my son at home, back in Russia," he said. He seemed upset. "I want to help you, Abdul."

I was very tired, and I had a headache.

"How can you help me?" I said. "The army is outside. We will both get into trouble. They will just kill us." I knew I had nothing to lose, as I was going to die anyway. But the doctor didn't need to be killed too. He seemed a nice man.

The doctor looked at me.

"I can help you," he said. "Rest now, and I will come back."

Before the doctor left, he sent me for an x-ray. My finger was broken in two places, at the lower knuckle and the middle knuckle. The cuts on my face and body were cleaned and bandaged by nurses, and I was given some water to drink and biscuits to eat. My swollen head was bandaged, but I still couldn't think above the headache. I felt very sick.

For the next two days I lay in the bed recovering from my injuries. The Russian doctor resisted every attempt to have me sent back to the prison. Nurses came in to change my bandages. I ate well in the hospital, better than I had in months. Slowly I began to feel a bit stronger.

On the third night, the doctor woke me, speaking very quietly. "You have to listen to me very carefully, Abdul. I am going to smuggle you out in my car. They never check the boot, and anyway I have paid some money to make sure."

He gave me a cleaner's overalls.

"Put these on. When you are dressed, empty the bin and take the bin bag outside the building to where you see my car. Look out for the security camera. You have five minutes to get into the boot. One of the cleaners will help you close it."

I looked at him.

"Why are you helping me?" I asked.

"You are a child, Abdul. You could be my son. If you stay here and keep refusing to do what they say, they are definitely going to kill you. You are very sick already."

I put the overalls on. I still didn't know whether to stay or go.

"What will happen to you?" I asked.

"Nothing," the doctor said. "People are smuggled out this way and many other ways all the time by the people smugglers. The prison will assume someone paid for you to be released."

He smiled at me standing there in the too-big uniform.

"Put this hat on," he said. "It will hide the bandage on your head."

I put on the hat.

"Good," he said. "Take that black binbag with you, and as soon as you have put it in the rubbish outside, get in the boot of the car. There will be a man there, he is safe. Keep behind him so the camera doesn't see you

– the man will close the boot." He smiled at me again. "Don't be frightened. You will be okay, and we will soon have you out of here."

I went outside with the bin bag and saw the jeep. A cleaner gestured to me and opened the boot. I climbed in with difficulty because of my aching limbs and head, and he closed it after me. I heard the engine start.

About 15 minutes later, the doctor opened the boot, flooding it with moonlight.

"I can't take you any further," he said. "The bus station is not far from here. Stay in your overalls. You're a man on your way home from work."

I climbed out. I didn't know how to thank him. I still couldn't think straight.

"You are free, Abdul," the doctor said. "I have to go. Go safely."

He drove off, leaving me standing there in the black night in my cleaner's overalls. I didn't know where to go or what to do. I started walking in the direction the doctor had indicated, keeping to the shadows. As a migrant worker I had no ID card, which would mean being sent straight back to jail. Even if I made it to the bus station, I knew I was still 100 miles or so from Ajdabiya. But I just kept putting one foot in front of the other on a road barely visible in the dark and the dust.

After a while, I managed to find a bus station. I found a quiet corner to rest for a while, waiting for the dawn to break. At first light, I found a minibus that said it was going north, towards the coast. I got on and spoke to the driver.

"I need to get to Ajdabiya," I said. I used my best Libyan accent and dialect. "But I have lost all my money. My relative will pay you at the other end."

The driver wasn't very happy, but he let me on. I looked very ill, and I suppose he wondered what a young boy was doing on his own so far from Ajdabiya.

"Do you have an ID card?" he asked.

"I've forgotten it," I said. "We Libyans need to remember our ID cards though, I know."

The driver drove like a madman, weaving through the traffic and playing chicken with bigger buses and blind corners, and so it only took a couple of hours to get back to Ajdabiya.

The driver told me to sit up at the front with him, and we chatted a lot of the way. He was a nice man. He shared his water and food with me, and he never knew I wasn't a Libyan boy going home. As we got into Ajdabiya I began worrying, but then I saw Ibrahim from our building and started waving. I couldn't believe it was him. He couldn't believe it either, when he saw me on the bus.

"Stop the bus!" I told the driver. "Here is my relative come to meet me!"

Luckily, Ibrahim had just enough money to pay the driver. He hugged me tightly when I got off the bus.

"What happened to your head, Abdul?" he asked. "I heard you were in prison. Aboud told me. You poor boy!"

I shook my head. I didn't want to talk about it.

Ibrahim brought me to the house and went and called all the family.

"Look who's here!" he said. "It's Abdul! Abdul has returned to us!"

Everyone was shocked to see me so battered and bruised, and so thin, but they were so happy to see me. Being back at that cramped flat felt like home. Even without Aboud, who was still working in Benghazi, I felt as if I was back with some kind of family.

The family sent to Benghazi for Aboud. He came home as soon as he could.

"I can't believe you are here, Abdul," he kept saying. "I can't believe you made it back to Ajdabiya."

I asked whether we could send now for Yusuf and Zeinab, but Aboud said that now wasn't safe with all the raids they were doing on the migrant quarters, and that there were fears of a civil war intensifying in the country.

I was impatient, but I didn't want to put Yusuf in more danger.

"We will send for them when it is safe," Aboud said.

The next day he had good news.

"I've spoken to my employer," he said. "He is a good man, and he has said I can move back to Ajdabiya to look after you. I can work at his tiling company. Even better, we can live in the building where they make the tiles. We'll have somewhere to live together."

Chapter Seven
Tripoli

It was wonderful to be back with Aboud in Ajdabiya, living above the tiling company. I slowly recovered from my injuries and the memory of being tortured began to fade; but the headaches from being beaten with the iron bar never stopped, even to this day, and my finger has never worked again. I also still bear a scar across my left knee where I was hit with the cosh.

Libya was suffering from its own painful scars. The country felt restless at that time. The numbers of armed men on the streets were increasing every day and it was never clear exactly whose side they were on. Of course, as illegal migrants, no-one was on your side. Gaddafi's men wanted to kill us or lock us up in case we joined the uprising that was said to be imminent. The rebels accused us of being mercenaries so desperate for money that we would fight for Gaddafi. As Africans, we knew that whatever kind of militia in camouflage uniform was coming towards you, the only thing to do was run.

Libya was awash with migrants from conflicts all over Africa. War and climate refugees funnelled up from unsafe countries and failed states. Mass migrations caused by droughts, famines and crop failures. Local conflicts aggravated by scarce resources. Before 2011, there were estimated to be one million illegal immigrants inside Libya, in a country with a total population of just six million people.

Ajdabiya was known to be one area where many lived, but there were entire districts of Tripoli that were home to Sudanese or Nigeriens from Niger, or Chadians. That year, 2010, Libya signed an agreement with the European Union to slow illegal migration between the two areas. When war returned, all of us − illegal immigrants, migrant workers, Africans passing through Libya − would be bottom of the pile.

When the Libyan Uprising finally happened on 17 February 2011 after 42 years of dictatorship under "Colonel" Muammar Gaddafi, as the gateway to Benghazi, Ajdabiya was right at its heart. One cool February day that week, I was walking down the street when I saw some men with a giant portrait of Colonel

Gaddafi, the kind that hung in all the government and official buildings, where he is in full military uniform and his chest is hung with medals. The men had thrown the portrait on the ground and were stamping on it until the glass cracked, kicking it until it was completely broken. Then they set fire to it, Gaddafi's face slowly disappearing under the flames. Only three years earlier, the Libyan leader had proclaimed himself the King of African Kings.

The Arab Spring was already spreading across the Middle East. Now, the security forces fired on peaceful pro-democracy protesters in Benghazi. As rebellion spread across the country like wildfire, government forces began killing civilians indiscriminately. The Brotherly Leader Colonel Gaddafi pledged to "purify the country, inch by inch, house by house, street by street, person by person", attacking demonstrators with tanks and artillery, and from the air. The UN established a no-fly zone over Libya that became a bombing campaign against military establishments.

From that moment onwards, we lived under siege and bombardment, attack and counter-attack. Gaddafi's troops were better equipped, better trained and better prepared than the rebels, but the rebels knew the city. Despised by both sides, our own allegiances – which had never been to the dictator Gaddafi – now became only to ourselves.

The rebels captured Ajdabiya early in the uprising, burning down the local government headquarters and declaring it a "Free City" by the end of March. A rebel stronghold surrounded by weapons dumps and oilfields, Gaddafi's forces were determined to bring the city quickly back under control.

At night, the place where I had begun to feel safe again since returning from prison was bombed by the security forces' fighter jets and helicopter gunships. The UN-authorised bombing planes thundered overhead. They were supposed to be protecting civilians, but often hit civilian targets in the city too. Huge oil fires blazed all around the city, thickening the air with black smoke. Fighters on all sides were heavily armed and waving the black, red and green flag. The sight of combatants praying in the street wrapped in the flag of Libya became a common sight.

I stopped sleeping again, lying in the dark listening to the bombs and gunfire. Our city became a blackened shell. The electricity and water supply stopped. There was no food, no more trips to the market, no more playing in the bombed-out streets. Ajdabiya was under rebel control, but completely surrounded and cut off by Gaddafi forces. Then, one night, Gaddafi's forces recaptured the town. Revenge was swift.

After that, things got very bad in Ajdabiya. People were dragged out of their houses and killed. NATO planes were busy at night bombing government tanks. Sometimes they missed their targets and hit civilians and houses. Schools and hospitals were closed because of unexploded mines. Slowly the city was emptying, with people moving out to encampments in the desert, or to stay with relatives, or just to get anywhere away from the city. Aboud and I were some of the only people left in our building.

As part of this exodus, many people were travelling west along the coast to Tripoli. It cost a lot of money to go because no-one wanted to undertake such a dangerous journey. Despite this, there were reports of huge numbers of people massing on the border with Tunisia and Egypt and in the ports, desperately trying to leave the country.

By now, the Red Cross had set up a big operation in Ajdabiya. They were feeding people too, and treating the sick in field hospitals. The government was repeatedly attacking their convoys. I made my way to their head-quarters and got a blanket, and some food.

I didn't know what to do, so I went to talk to the imam.

"There is no life for you here, any more, Abdul," he told me. "You must leave Ajdabaya. Maybe one day when it is peaceful, we can all return."

Aboud agreed we must go. I didn't even get to say goodbye to the children and the rest of the family I had lived with for so long in Ajdabiya. But perhaps they had already left too.

That afternoon we joined an exodus of thousands heading along the bombed-out road out of Ajdabiya. The coastal highway was clogged with retreating rebels, family cars piled high with possessions, and people walking, carrying all their worldly goods in their arms. Aboud thought we would be safer in Tripoli, where he still had contacts. Somehow we managed to get a lift in the back of a truck going that way.

Tripoli's skyline, though ravaged by war, still stood proudly above the rubble – a damaged muddle of luxury hotels, intricately carved minarets, Roman ruins, sand-coloured forts and vast squares lit up at night by rocket-fire.

The image of Colonel Gaddafi hung over the city in the form of a giant mural in Green Square, later named Martyrs' Square. Buildings were missing their faces, as if their fronts had slid off into the street. Gaddafi souvenirs were still being sold in the marketplace even as anti-Gaddafi leaflets fell like autumn leaves from the skies.

Aboud managed to find the family he had lived with before, and they said we could stay until we found somewhere to live. Aboud got some labouring work, and I found some work for a while as a domestic servant for an Italian family. I had to be there every day before dawn and clean their whole house from top to bottom, which would take several hours. They didn't really speak to me, and I was too shy to speak to them, but I used to listen to their Italian voices. One of the older children taught me a few words, and when they saw me staring at the map on the kitchen wall, they showed me the different countries. I liked the sound of Italian, the way it sounded like singing compared with the harder sounds of Arabic.

My getting a job at least meant we could buy some food, even if there wasn't very much available in the shops. Tripoli was better than Ajdabiya to begin with, but under its hard blue skies we could feel the contagion of war slowly begin to take a stronger grip.

The Battle of Tripoli began in August, when just after Iftar, the meal that breaks the Ramadan fast, the rebels launched Operation Mermaid Dawn, a codename that came from Libyans' nickname for their city, "The Mermaid". Helped by information from Gaddafi's caterer who had defected, rebels even overwhelmed the dictator's fortress residence in the city, sending him into hiding. Bakers in Tripoli began making sweets in the colours of the rebel flag.

We ventured out again only to learn that as usual it made little difference to us. Rumours still abounded that Gaddafi had flown in African mercenaries to attack rebels, meaning every African was now under suspicion. There was no side African migrants were safe with in this civil war.

In those days of bombing and shelling, when the soundtrack to our lives was constant shouts and explosions, I was no longer afraid of dying, because I had nothing to live for apart from some instinctive idea that I should stay alive.

Our daily existence was just trying to find scraps of food and to dodge snipers and the armed trucks joyriding around the city, shooting anything that moved. There were frequent water shortages, and finding water became the most difficult thing of all.

We no longer had any way of feeding ourselves, so the only food we ate came from the mosque. I now told everyone that I was Libyan but I had lost my ID card. Rations were only available to Libyans even at the mosque.

Meanwhile, every day more migrants were being taken off to makeshift prisons springing up all over Libya. Stories came of black African men being rounded up in Tripoli, accused of being *mortzaga*, or mercenaries, fighting for Colonel Gaddafi. What had begun as mass xenophobia was becoming a murderous excuse for mass detentions and mass executions.

In the heat of late August 2011, rebel soldiers came to our apartment block, which housed only African migrant families. They arrived out of nowhere, men with heavy guns and bullet belts dressed in black or wearing unmatching camouflage uniforms. Men in flipflops, berets and baseball caps. One man carried a megaphone, which he used to call to the whole building.

"All men over 15 must come out now," they said. "If we find any men who have not come out, it will be the worse for all of you."

We were all hiding inside the apartment, shutters covering the windows, lying on the floor.

"Come out now, or we will kill everyone in the building," the soldier with the megaphone said.

Aboud got up from his hiding place. He didn't fight back. He just went. I don't remember that he said goodbye.

He walked down to the bottom of the building with the other men. There was an open truck, and the soldiers threw him in with all the others – men from the fields, men from the houses, every African man of fighting age.

Aboud did it to save us. He saved our lives. The soldiers went from door to door after that, and they bombed any apartment that hadn't sent its men down. In those families, they killed the man, the wife, the daughters, the sons, the elderly people, everybody. They checked every single room and bedroom. I watched them throwing the men in the truck.

Hundreds of men, mainly African migrants, were executed by firing squad in Tripoli during that week. I don't know if Aboud was among them, but I never saw him again.

A newspaper leader from August 30 laments of the rebel fighters that "the original emancipatory impulse of 17 February lies, for now, among the corpses of 'Africans' in Tripoli."

All I knew was that the kind and gentle man who had lost his own family, and dedicated the rest of his life to saving mine, was lost that week to murderous madness. Aboud, my father's best friend, who had brought me thousands of miles to Libya, through Chad, all the way from Darfur. A man who had survived the attack on his village, a disease-ravaged refugee camp, people-traffickers and slave labour, was taken away in silence, thrown in a truck and driven away. The last connection I had to my family was scratched out, and I was overwhelmed by loss.

After that, the killing never seemed to stop. By late summer, there were bodies of alleged collaborators lying bloated all over the hot streets. There seemed to be flies everywhere, covering the bodies, in the air, in our tiny apartment.

Tripoli was grey with dust from the constant shelling and bombardment, and its alleyways were a river of death and sewage. The number of casualties on both sides seemed unending.

At one point, I was trapped in the flat for three weeks without leaving, watching the tiny food supplies Aboud and I had built up together dwindling, eating only a mouthful or two a day. I couldn't even go out of the front door because of all the shooting, and all of the unexploded bombs lying in the streets. I knew if I stepped outside, I would be dead, or, if I was caught, God knows, a fate worse than death awaited me.

I was trapped in the flat but terrified of being there, expecting any moment that the soldiers would return for those they had spared. When there was a break in the shelling one day, I decided to run and head for another part of Tripoli that might be less targeted by fighters. I hoped to find some food somewhere in the city's bins, or on the shelves of a looted supermarket.

I came across a bombed-out building in the city where other migrants were staying. They welcomed me in. We were all in the same situation, hiding from the authorities, hungry and exhausted. The battle-scarred building had a roof and some running water. The migrants had dragged a few blankets and chairs inside.

Every day we would go out onto the streets and find the bodies of our dead brothers and sisters. We would dig graves and try to bury them, and say a small prayer over them. We would imagine they were our parents or our brothers or our friends, and try to treat them as we'd hope our beloved people would be treated. One of the boys was called Khaled. He was a homeless Libyan boy who had become separated from his family. He showed me how to scavenge in bins for food, and find the emergency food distributions carried out by aid agencies. Then we went home to half sleep in the bombed-out building, our hands pressed over our ears.

Towards the end of Ramadan that year, Khaled and the others from the building said they were moving to Benghazi. They had heard things were better there and that there were boats taking people – even African migrants – to safety in Italy and other parts of Europe. I had no feeling about whether that was a bad or good idea, and no real desire to go to Europe, or to go anywhere, but most of all I feared being on my own in the middle of all of this horror.

Now I no longer had Aboud, this group of homeless migrants was all I had. They told me the imam at the local mosque was organising safe passage for Africans from Tripoli to Benghazi.

"You must come, Abdul," Khaled said. "Before you are rounded up."

My Libyan accent was almost as good as his, and I knew I could mainly pass as Libyan, but I had no papers if the rebels came for me, and no family or friends left to care.

The journey to Benghazi meant travelling all the way back past Ajdabiya, along the Libyan coast. The roads were in total chaos, fleeing families packed into trucks and cars heading one way or another along the coast road. Every traveller had to negotiate mortar attacks, road blocks and random security searches. Above us at night, the sky lit up with NATO bombers and distant rocket fire.

When we reached Benghazi in late August 2011, the whole city was in chaos. The port was packed with thousands of people desperate to be evacuated to safety. The main evacuations were coming from Misrata, but some of the boats were docking at Benghazi to take foreign nationals out of the country. Every time a new boat appeared on the horizon, the whole port seemed to surge forward towards the sea.

Migrant workers were among those being officially evacuated, and the port was full of Tunisians, Moroccans, Somalis,
Eritreans and other African nationalities, all clamouring to
climb on board a ship to safety. Hundreds were carrying their
belongings in bulging suitcases, cardboard boxes and bin bags
tied up with string. Others were completely empty-handed,
having escaped only with their clothes and empty pockets.

The docks were full of the biggest ships I had ever seen.
Among them was a cruise ship, the size of a town. It had
four floors and could fit 3,000 people on board. People were
desperate to get on board these ships, but I had no documents
and no way of stowing away on one.

I made my way to the local mosque with Khaled and the
migrants who had come from Tripoli. It was the only place
we could think of to go for food. When they moved on to try
to get onto a boat, I stayed at the mosque because I was too
frightened to go with them. The imam was very kind to me. I
was completely alone and he could see I was afraid. I was 14
by then, but I have always looked young for my age.

Imam Mohammed's young son Ibrahim had been shot.
He needed a hospital, but all the clinics in Benghazi had
been shelled or had run out of medicines.

"I don't know what to do, Abdul," he told me. "I should
stay in Benghazi with my mosque, but my son needs to go
to Europe."

On the fourth day, Imam Mohammed called me to him.

"I've got a place on a hospital ship for Ibrahim," he said. "I don't want to leave my country, but I have to do what I can for my son."

I nodded. By now I was used to the fact that every friend I made died or moved on, one way or another.

"Abdul, you must come too," he said. "You can't stay here. You are a minor, you are a foreign national. Foreigners are leaving this town every day."

"I have no money," I told him. "I have nothing."

"I will sort it out, Abdul," he said. "Leave it to me."

The next morning, we went down to the port with the other people being evacuated. The streets were packed with people desperate to leave the country. The crowds were so big and kept pushing forwards until it felt like they were going to fall into the harbour.

The imam was carrying his young, injured son in his arms.

"Just stick close to me," he said.

The big white cruise ship was waiting. I was very nervous getting on board. It was like a giant hotel. There were bedrooms with televisions, doctors, a huge restaurant. Injured people were being treated in every corridor. They were taking children and foreign nationals, women and injured people.

I got on with Imam Mohammed and he went off with Ibrahim to the hospital wing. I pushed open the door of an empty cabin and crawled into the bed. It had soft bed linen and I slept for a while. When I woke up, I saw there was a bathroom attached to the cabin with expensive tiles and taps. I washed my face and looked at myself in the mirror. My hair was bigger that it had ever been in my life, huge and matted, and made bigger by the cheekbones jutting out of my hollow cheeks. My eyes were reddened by dust and clouded by the things they had seen. I went out of the cabin and went to stand out on deck watching Libya disappear, and the edge of the African continent fading to a dark line in the distance. The sun was warm on my face, and the wind cold as the boat ploughed on through the dark waves.

Chapter Eight
France

The journey took two days and two nights across raging seas. After the first hour or so when we were near to the coast, the vessel began to rock violently, sending everyone to find a cabin. I was frequently sick, but I still managed to eat the food served for free in the boat's dining rooms three times a day. I couldn't remember the last time I had had breakfast, lunch and dinner. I crammed the food into my mouth.

I had never been on a boat before in all of my long journey, and the ocean was both fascinating and terrifying to me. So black and deep and unending, but yet so clean and empty. After the noise of war and the stench of the bodies in the street, even the cloying smell of the diesel engine felt sterile and the white noise of boat and waves was calming, drowning out even my nightmares. I took a shower in the cabin and put my ragged, filthy clothes back on. At night, I woke up rolling in the big white bed and had no idea where I was.

It was late at night when we eventually arrived in a huge French port two days later. In the moonlight, I could see there was a beautiful mountain behind the docks, and very many houses and blocks of flats. A huge city tumbling down to the sea.

It was a warm night and as the boat came into the harbour, we all stood on deck watching the twinkling lights of France growing brighter.

The man next to me squeezed my shoulder.

"Look at that!" he said. "No bombs. No guns. Europe!"

It might sound crazy, but I've never worked out what French port that ferry came in to. It must have been somewhere on the southern coast of France. It could have been Nice or Toulon, but it seems most likely it was Marseille. One day, when I have a passport, I will go and look along the coast and see where it was I lived.

All I know is that when we got off the boat we were told to go straight in a line, not left or right, but straight onto the bus at the end of the road. As soon as the bus was full, it went and another one arrived. It was a long queue to get off the ship, and by the time we reached dry land, it was the middle of the night, but the port was still busy with people loading and unloading and boats coming in and out.

The buses took us to a hotel, but when we got there it was a very long time before we could check in to our rooms, and they didn't seem to have a record of most of our names. They seemed to have no idea who had been on the boat. Next to the people working in the hotel, my clothes felt very dirty and ragged. I wondered how we must look to them.

Some of the men wanted to go to the mosque to thank God for delivering them safely across the sea to a country without war. I wanted to pray and give thanks too. I was still afraid, and completely on my own in a strange country. But the man's words rang in my head: no bombs, no guns.

I set off with the men and we walked for an hour to the mosque. We got lost many times on the way, but after a while we could see the minaret calling us. When we reached the mosque, the imam let us in despite it still being the middle of the night, and we all found something deeply comforting in the act of praying, laying our foreheads down on the cool floor of a French mosque in a country we knew nothing about.

Afterwards, I walked back with some of the same group of men, but we were completely disorientated in the dark. Soon we were lost again. None of us knew how to get back, and none of us spoke French to get directions from anybody. We went back to the mosque and asked if we could sleep there. Dozens of refugees from Libya and other countries were already sleeping there or sitting at green-painted tables, so we joined them.

The next day we managed to find the hotel again, but they said they had no record of us. We had no ID cards and no paperwork.

"How do we know you came on the boat?" an official asked us. "You might have come from anywhere."

"We will have to starve in the street," a man said.

The official told us to report to the police station, but there was no way I was going to hand myself in. I had no idea if they would torture us or send us back to Libya.

We went back to the mosque, but there were too many people there. Someone told us to go to the park, as lots of refugees slept there. The night felt bitterly cold for all those of us who had spent so many nights in the Sahara. We tried the local church and they gave us some food, but said we couldn't sleep there.

It was late August in France, hot in the day but cold at night, especially to someone used to the dry burning heat of North Africa. I tried sleeping on a bench, and then I tried sleeping in some bushes. I couldn't find anywhere to get warm. This was the first of many nights I spent in the park, and soon became part of a routine. In the daytime, we went to the church or the mosque for food and to just spend time sitting somewhere safe. At night, the park.

France was safer than Libya, but I couldn't speak or read the language, and I was hungry, cold and completely alone. I made some friends at the mosque, but I must have looked completely crazy. My hair was long and very curly and matted and I was so thin. I was in filthy clothes and still in my slippers from Libya. My feet were so cold.

The mosque was full of Algerians and Tunisians. A lot of the talk was about how to leave the city. "There are too many people here, and nowhere to go," they said. "We can't all of us live in one park. We need to go to other places."

I made some friends there, but then, suddenly, they would leave. Some went to Calais, some went to other countries. Everyone seemed to know where they were going.

The summer ended abruptly, the park turned brown and yellow, and even the birds began migrating south. At the mosque that October, some Libyans told me Colonel Gaddafi had been captured hiding in a large drainage pipe and killed by the rebels. Autumn became winter. It started snowing on and off. On the second night it snowed, I couldn't bear it any longer. I saw a big commercial bin, and I knew if I climbed in it would keep the snow off me, and it would be warmer. I climbed in. It stank of rubbish, and the sweet smell almost made me vomit. But it was warm and dry, and the bin bags inside were a kind of cushion. After that I started sleeping in the bin every night. I stopped smelling the bin, probably because I myself now smelled like the inside of a bin, with nowhere to wash my filthy clothes.

In the park, I made a friend called Walid. He was an older Tunisian man. He used to sit in the park with his grandchildren while they played. I liked to talk to him. He was a good listener, and he spoke Arabic. Over the weeks I had told him probably more than any other person about my life. My family in Darfur, our journey through Chad, living through the war in Libya. Walid had been in France a long time, escaping political repression and poverty in his homeland.

"Hello, my son," he said when he saw me. "Are you still here? Last night, I looked for you, but I didn't see you. Where did you go?"

"I am living in a bin now," I said.

Walid was upset by that.

"I wish I could bring you to my house, but I only live in one room and I have a wife and two children," he said.

I nodded my head.

"I can't bring you to live with me, but I tell you what I will do. Every day I will bring you a sandwich."

After that, Walid brought me a sandwich every day. A tuna sandwich. French people make nice bread and have good tuna, and Walid made good sandwiches. I think that, for a long while, that man and those tuna sandwiches were the only thing keeping me alive.

One early morning when I was sleeping in the bin, I woke up to feel it moving. At first, I didn't understand what was happening, but then I realised the dustbin lorry must have come to empty the bin. I was very frightened, as I'd seen what happened to the bins when they were emptied into the jaws of a great big bin lorry, the rubbish crushed instantly between its teeth.

I began hammering on the side of the bin as hard as I could. I couldn't tell if anyone could hear me. The lorry's engine and the machinery lifting the bin were very loud. I kept banging and banging. The bin kept swinging upwards until it was almost completely upside down. I was flung against the lid, shouting until I was hoarse.

Then the movement suddenly stopped. I could hear voices shouting outside. After a while I heard a fire engine siren.

It took a long time before they managed to open the bin. A man spoke to me in French, but I couldn't understand him. I replied in Arabic. After a while, a different man came and spoke to me in Arabic. He said he was a translator, from Tunisia.

"The police and the fire brigade are trying to get you out," he said. "It's very difficult because they don't want to crush you."

"Okay," I said.

"What are you doing in this bin?"

"I had nowhere to go," I said. "I was very cold."

"What is your name?"

"Abdul," I said.

"Any papers?"

"No," I said.

They brought a big cutting machine and it took a long time to free me, but eventually, they got the bin down to the ground, and I could get out. My teeth were chattering, and I couldn't stop shivering. My head was aching badly again. I felt very strange, and I couldn't remember ever having been so cold.

The police wrapped me in a silver blanket and gave me some water to sip.

"They are sending you to the church," the translator said, "while they get hold of social services. Don't worry. They will help you. You are only a young boy."

When we got to the church, the priest took me to a meeting room. He was very kind. He said his name was Monsignor Antonio. A lady brought me some blankets and they helped me wrap myself in them. They brought me some orange juice to drink – it tasted beautiful, so sweet. I drank it very quickly. Then the lady brought me a cheese sandwich. I can still taste how delicious it was.

Monsignor Antonio came back with some socks and shoes to replace my slippers, and some worn but soft clothes. He looked at my crazy hair, and said I could have a shower. He was very tall and smartly dressed, with a white collar and a light blue robe.

He went to find someone from the church who could speak Arabic. He came back with someone who looked African.

"You are freezing cold, Abdul," the man said. "Maybe you have hypothermia?"

He sent for some more blankets and asked if they could build a fire.

"Where are your family?" he asked me.

"They are all dead, apart from my brother Yusuf," I said. "And I don't know where he is."

"Are you from Libya?"

"Darfur," I said. "I came through Chad to Libya."

The man looked amazed at my journey.

"You have come a long way," he said.

He spoke to the priest for a while.

"Do you want to make a claim for asylum in France?" he asked me, eventually.

"I don't know anyone here," I said. "I am completely alone. But I don't have any other home. My home in Darfur was burned down and I would rather die than go back to Libya."

"So, you want to be French?"

"I don't know anything about France," I said.

"The problem is the bin collector has called the police," the man said. "So, we will have to do something official."

I started to panic that they might take me to jail. I was very frightened of prison after going to jail in Libya.

"Can you let me go?" I said. I was taking the blanket off me and looking around for my shoes. "I need to go. I won't get into any trouble again."

The priest was speaking to me, but I couldn't understand him. I asked the man to translate.

"He says we can't have a child sleeping in a bin. You can stay here for a few days while we work something out. We will deal with the authorities."

I stayed at the church four or five days, but I couldn't relax. I kept thinking the police were coming for me, so I went to try and find my friends from the park at the mosque. They had all gone. An old man told me they had all gone to Calais or to try their luck at the lorry park.

I went to the park to see if anyone was left there. Walid was there with his grandchildren.

"Where have you been?" he asked me. "I've been worried about you." He laughed. "I've had to eat all your sandwiches."

I told him about the bin being emptied with me inside it. Walid shook his head with horror, and then began to laugh.

"I've heard it all now, Abdul," he said.

Then he looked at me more seriously.

"What's happened to all your friends?" Walid said.

"They are all gone," I said.

"Why don't you go too?" he said.

I explained I didn't have any money, not even one coin to pay traffickers, and I didn't know how to jump the lorries. I was going to sleep in the park for the rest of my life or maybe die of the cold.

Walid shook his head.

"Look Abdul, I can help you," he said.

I tried to protest.

"No money. Just as a friend. Let me help you." He shook his head. "We can't have you living in a bin."

Chapter Nine
The Lorry

Walid wasn't able to help me for a few days. He had to make the necessary arrangements, he said. In the meantime, I just kept on sleeping in the park and going to the mosque or the church in the day for food. I still wasn't sure about his plan, but I knew I couldn't endure another winter sleeping in a bin. The city's beautiful, lamp-lit centre gave way to dark and dangerous northern districts that were awash with poverty and drug violence. Migrants were sometimes attacked or robbed by drunken groups of young men.

Through 2011 and 2012, more and more migrants were arriving by sea or across the mountainous border with Italy as a result of the crisis in Libya. We were often blamed for the city's problems and often moved on by the police. Sometimes mass arrests were made, and migrants held for a night or two. I remained so terrified of the police that I kept away from busy streets and bright lights.

Then, in the early hours of a warm July morning, before even the birds had begun singing, Walid came and found me in the park as arranged. He drove me in his battered car to a big industrial estate just outside the city where lorries were emptied and loaded. He had no problem getting into the lorry park, where sleeping vehicles stretched in every direction.

Keeping low, we looked for ones with an English number plate or GB written on them. Walid knew to knock on the side of the lorry to see if it was empty or loaded, ready to go.

Eventually, he found the lorry he was looking for.

"Okay, Abdul, you need to empty your bladder," he said.

"No thank you," I said.

I felt embarrassed to do it in front of Walid, and dirty to do it in the car park.

"Abdul, don't be silly. Do it quickly. You will be many hours without a toilet."

Walid brought a holdall out of the boot, and unpacked it. He gave me a thick, green padded jacket, some heavy gloves, and socks to put on over my own tattered pair. I put all the clothing on. Walid gave me some biscuits and told me to zip them into my jacket pocket.

"Do you have any water?" I asked.

"No water," Walid said. "You'll need the toilet. It's best to go with no water."

For a moment I hesitated. My body felt poised to run away.

"People pay thousands of euros to make this journey," Walid said, into my ear. "I'm helping you to go for free. This might be your last chance to find freedom. I've lived in this city a long time, and I've seen what happens to boys like you who stay living in that park. I'm telling you there is nothing to stay for, and there is no way back. Now let's go!"

I was frightened.

"What if I fall?"

"You will die," Walid said. "But you won't fall."

Walid pulled me under the lorry. We both had to duck down to get underneath. He shone his torch beam up into the blackness above the wheels, where there was a tiny, dark space.

I climbed up, using the axle to pull my body into position.

There was just enough space to hide, if I folded my body up. I could balance using my hands and feet on top of the wheel arches. It wasn't uncomfortable, at least while the vehicle wasn't moving – certainly no more or less comfortable than lying on a piece of cardboard in the park.

Walid told me to hold on tight to the metal – that was why he had given me the gloves.

"Do not fall," he said. "I mean it, Abdul. Do not let go. Do not fall asleep. Just keep holding on. And do not get off until you are sure the lorry has fully stopped, and you have heard the driver get out. That's how most people die. Listen for the door closing and wait a few minutes longer. Be sure."

He passed me up some chocolate from his pocket.

"I'm frightened," I blurted out. I hadn't meant to say it.

"Just trust in God," Walid said. "Think of everything you have done. You have survived a war in Sudan. You've been through a war in Libya. You've escaped from Chad. Don't be scared. So many people have done this before you, and so many have survived and made a new life. When you got on the boat, it was dangerous, but God protected you. Think of everything that has passed and everything that has happened to you and have faith."

I watched Walid's torch disappear under the lorry, leaving me in total blackness. I held on where he had showed me and waited for my eyes to adjust to the absence of light. I heard Walid tap twice on the lorry, and then his footsteps walking away.

"Goodbye, Abdul," the tap seemed to say.

I tried to pull myself together.

"This is a good lorry," I thought to myself. "I've got a lucky seat. I've got chocolate and biscuits. I've got nothing to lose."

I sat there for about an hour, shivering. It was very cold, even in my new warm jacket. I thought about England. I had no idea what it was like there. A lot of other people had gone there, so I thought it must be nice.

So far, in France, I was sleeping in a bin, I had no friends and I was hungry and cold every day. I was very tired, and I began to fall asleep.

I heard the engine starting up and I tried to remember what Walid had told me. "Trust in God." I put a square of chocolate into my mouth and tightened my grip through the gloves onto the metal. The lorry started moving.

The next hours were cold and windy as the winds whistled through the underside of the lorry. The roads were winding at first, throwing me around, but then we got onto long straight roads for what seemed like hours. It was a strange feeling to be moving so fast, flying along the motorways. Gradually the world outside got lighter and I could see the road beneath whipping past, a dizzying river of grey motorway. It seemed as if the whole world smelled of petrol.

My legs were so stiff they began to burn and my back ached, but I still kept gripping on how Walid had showed me. I tried to force my eyes to stay open against the tempting lull of the vehicle and the strong desire for sleep.

After a while, it went very dark and the lorry stopped. For half an hour it was very, very noisy, but warmer, with no rushing air. It was a curious feeling because there was no sound from the engine and the wheels of the lorry weren't moving but I still felt as if we were moving along. I allowed myself to stop gripping onto the metal in front of me and prepared to run. This might be the moment they would catch me, while we had stopped. I wanted to run but I remembered Walid's words to listen for the driver leaving the vehicle.

My head ached, and I let my forehead rest briefly on the metal, wondering where we were and what would happen next.

I awoke abruptly when the engine was re-started and the lorry started moving again. We came out into the light and I saw it was still daytime. The lorry started slowly but the road started blurring faster and faster beneath me. Had that been the tunnel Walid had told me about, I wondered? Were we now in England?

When the lorry eventually stopped it was night again, and I didn't know what to do. My body was very stiff and cold, and I couldn't move. I heard dogs barking, then something grabbed my foot with its mouth. A torch shone in my face. I heard some shouting in a language I didn't understand. Gloved hands pulled me out from under the lorry and kept me down on the floor. I saw two security guards and two dogs. I didn't know what was going to happen to me. I couldn't be sure if I was still in France or if I had made it to England. Perhaps I was in another country altogether, Italy or Belgium?

One of the men shone a torch in my face, and they let me up. I couldn't understand what they were saying, but they seemed to have softened. Perhaps they could see I was only a child.

The police arrived quickly. They didn't look like French police, and had different uniforms.

They were speaking a language I didn't know, which I hoped was English.

They started leading me towards a police car and I realised we were going to a police station. I suddenly started to panic. These police might take me to a locked room and torture me again. They might beat me and throw me onto the streets or return me to Sudan.

I was very frightened then and I wanted to run away. I tried to run into the road, to be run down by a car, but the police grabbed me and put me in the car instead. I couldn't resist because my legs were very stiff from being under the lorry and I felt very weak and tired. My head was banging with a headache.

"What country?" I asked in Arabic, and then in French, but no-one could understand me.

The police car took us along the motorway to a big modern building made of glass and lit up against the night sky. A policewoman with a kind face took me to a room and brought a translator. The translator spoke to me in French.

"I'm not French," I said. "I'm Sudanese. From Darfur."

The translator spoke to me in Arabic. She said she was from Jordan.

"What is your name?" she asked.

"Abdul," I said. "Where am I, please?"

"You are in England," the translator said. "At Gablecross Police Station, in a town called Swindon. You are being detained by Wiltshire Police on suspicion of immigration offences."

I felt very, very alone.

The policewoman brought me a cup of hot tea and some biscuits. I crammed the biscuits in my mouth. The sugary tea was delicious. I was so thirsty, and it was warm.

They asked me a lot of questions, which all had to be translated. I was very, very tired, and just wanted to sleep. I rested my head on the table.

"How old are you Abdul?" the policewoman asked.

"I'm not sure," I said. "What year is it now?"

The translator smiled kindly.

"2012."

"I'm 15," I said.

"What year did you leave Darfur?"

"2004."

"Are you sure?"

I nodded. "Of course."

"You have been on the road for eight years?"

"Yes, I think so," I said.

"Where have you been in that time?"

"My home was burned down in Darfur. I walked to Chad, I stayed in Chad in a refugee camp, I went to Libya," I said. "Then I went to France."

The translator conveyed all this to the policewoman.

"Is there anything you'd like to ask us?"

"Could I have a sandwich, please?" I said.

The two women laughed.

"When is the last time you ate?" the translator asked.

"When I was in France. I think that was two days ago, but I don't know."

"What was the last thing you ate?"

"A tuna sandwich. And a piece of chocolate."

I drank more of the tea. I could feel it warming me slowly.

"Did you come from Calais, Abdul?"

I shook my head.

"I don't think so. I know some other people went there. They were always talking about Calais, but I didn't go there."

My lack of knowledge about the last part of my journey has been a frustration for the authorities ever since, but I genuinely have never known exactly where I came from. It was a busy French port with mountains behind and lots of white buildings on the southern coast of France. My best guess remains Marseille.

The road journey from Marseille to Swindon by lorry is around 15 hours, including travelling through the Channel Tunnel. How I could have possibly clung on for that long under a lorry I don't know. I remember so little of the journey. The memories that remain are fear, the feeling of motion, and the cold.

In my life now, people often think that the time I spent under the lorry was the most important part of my journey to the UK, but I can't weigh up the different components. In many ways sitting there in the quiet for all those hours was the easy part. Of course, had I let go I would just be another news story, like the Kenyan man who a few years later fell from the landing gear of an aeroplane into someone's garden in London while they were dozing in a deckchair. This is how people's lives happen in parallel. Someone is making the most desperate journey of their life while another person is sunbathing.

Chapter Ten
Wiltshire

After they brought me a sandwich to eat, the police-woman sent for a social worker. I went to the cells for a while to sleep. They told me I was safe and that nothing bad would happen to me. I didn't believe them, but I couldn't stop myself sleeping as soon as I lay down on the hard bench.

The social worker told me his name was Chris. When he arrived, I saw the time was 8.30am. I must have been in the police station all night.

Chris seemed a kind person. He asked me a few questions. He wrote that I had nothing with me, just the clothes I was standing up in. A yellow T-shirt and blue sweatshirt. Green padded jacket, tracksuit bottoms, socks, trainers. His notes say that I cried when I spoke about my family. I was very thin. My medical notes say I weighed just seven stone.

"What do you need?" he asked me.

Chris's notes say I replied: "Go to school, protection from the UK, live like any human being in peace without fear."

Chris drove me to a big house in Swindon old town, where an African lady answered the door. I was shaking with tiredness, and my head ached.

"You won't have to be here very long," Chris told me. "It's just somewhere to be safe while we find you a placement with a family."

The lady took me to a freezing cold room that had a bed, a cooker, and a fridge in it. I got into the bed and slept. She gave me a telephone number to ring if I needed her for anything and showed me a pay phone in the hallway. She gave me some coins to use in the telephone.

When I woke up, I looked in the fridge, but I didn't know what to do with any of the food in it. I drank all the milk in the doorway. I was too scared to go and talk to anyone.

After a while, I went out of the room and met a man who said he was from Afghanistan. He spoke strange Arabic.

"I don't know what to do with the food," I said. "I'm very hungry."

The man made me some rice and chicken in his room and brought it for me to eat.

"You'll get the hang of it," he said.

I'm not sure how much time passed. I was very tired and confused. But then social services said they were moving me to a temporary foster home with a couple who could be like my parents.

Chris brought me to the house in Swindon late in the evening, a few days later. I was apprehensive about meeting the couple, Lesley and Graham. What would they be like? Would they like me? What kind of food would they eat? Would they be Muslim or Christian? And how would we communicate if they didn't speak Arabic?

They lived in a nice warm house in the countryside. When they opened the front door, light spilled out onto the garden path. But the moment I entered the house, I felt myself tighten up inside, and my head began aching sharply where the scar from the iron bar is. In the hallway was a large black dog. In my culture, and some parts of Islam, black dogs are a very bad sign. Growing up, I was always told they can harbour evil. The elders even told me black dogs can subtract from some of the prayers and good deeds a person does each day – so it's necessary to say extra prayers and do extra good deeds if you see one.

As soon as I saw that black dog, I knew I couldn't live in that house. The couple, who were quite elderly, were very kind and they seemed as if they were nice, but I couldn't speak to them. I was too frightened. I would rather have been back on the streets living in the bin than stay in that house any longer. It didn't make sense, because in all those years I had dreamed only of being in a warm family home with food on the table and friends.

After Chris left, Lesley and Graham offered me some food. They had prepared a meal for me, but I couldn't eat it. My head was aching, and I couldn't look at them. I could only keep watching the door in case the dog came in. I thought about running away. I felt unclean because I knew the dog had been eating in the kitchen. I went to wash my hands many times, and then I said I had to go to bed.

They gave me some fresh, clean pyjamas and I put them on and lay on my bed staring at the ceiling, listening to the sound of the dog padding outside, the sound of its paws and claws on the wooden floor. The bed was too soft and after a while, I climbed down onto the floor and slept there, pulling the blankets down after me and over my head.

The next few days and weeks were very bad. I couldn't eat. I couldn't sleep. I became very anxious. At night, dreams of my family dead in the fire came into my mind, or I dreamed of being beaten in Libya. It was almost as though my brain had waited until I was safe to torture me with memories of what I had come through.

During the daytime, I had to have lots of interviews with social workers and doctors and psychiatrists. I told them everything. About the man who snapped my fingers in Libya. How they beat me in prison with an iron bar. About my dead family.

Lesley and Graham arranged days out for me, but I wouldn't go if the dog was going, and my headaches were so bad I often just lay on the cool pillow in the bedroom staring at the clean wall. I had so very little English I found it completely exhausting trying to speak to people and understand what they meant. There was so much noise in my head, I could hardly pick out a word anyone was saying.

Lesley and Graham were very kind, but their house didn't feel like a family house, like some of the ones I lived in in Libya when I was an illegal immigrant. Those houses were packed with families, kids of all ages and lots of adults, noise and laughter. Even though we never had enough food, and we were always frightened of the authorities coming to take us away, we all shared something in common. I wished that Lesley and Graham had other children who I could play with, and who could be my friends.

We went to a barbecue and I heard, to my joy, someone speaking Italian. It was such a lovely sound. I'd spoken a few words of Italian sometimes in Libya, and it was lovely to hear someone speaking a familiar language.

I went up to the Italian woman and spoke to her. She looked shocked to see the young refugee speaking to her, but we chatted for a while.

"I didn't know you spoke Italian," Graham said.

I wanted to tell him about when I was a servant for the Italian family in Libya, but I didn't have the words to tell him. I wished Lesley and Graham spoke Italian, because I didn't feel like I would ever be able to learn English.

Chapter Eleven
Swindon

Lesley and Graham took me to New College in Swindon where I was enrolled as a student to study ESOL – English to Speakers of Other Languages. I was absolutely terrified and felt sick all morning. My headache was very bad by the time we arrived. In my whole life, I had never, ever gone to school. Where I lived in Darfur, no children went to school. We boys were needed to work with the animals, and the girls were needed to fetch firewood and water. In Chad, the refugee camp sometimes had a school, but I never went there. It was a long walk away from where our makeshift shelter was, and I was needed there too – to look after Yusuf and help Zeinab while Aboud was at work.

In Libya, I was either left alone for long hours or I was working as a servant in the houses we lived in, and there was no way an illegal immigrant could go to school. In France, I was illegal and living in a bin or in the park. The kind priest asked me about going to school but I didn't want him to tell the authorities about me because I was frightened.

Now, after all these years, here I was going to my first ever day at school at the age of 15.

New College is on the edge of Swindon, surrounded by trees and green space. The buildings are enormous, like a spaceship. There is a huge car park at the front and the building has huge glass windows. Over 5,000 pupils go to New College, most of them over 16. On the first day, they told us they have libraries, computer rooms, dark rooms, lecture theatres, a sports hall, chemical labs, a recording studio. I didn't know what most of those things were for and I was already exhausted from listening to people speak English. I didn't speak myself in case people laughed at me.

My class had a lot of other refugees and teenagers who couldn't speak English, so we couldn't even speak to each other. I told the teachers I didn't understand the point of being there.

At break-time, I tried to hide myself from the crowds of young people laughing and joking and kicking footballs. There was so much noise, students charging past to get to lessons, people greeting their friends, teachers telling us things I didn't understand. I just wanted the noise to stop.

My headache got very bad and in the end I just put my head on the desk. A teacher said I could get some water if I needed to.

She asked me what I was interested in, but I just shook my head. How could I be interested in something I didn't understand? I told her I didn't want to come here again, but she said in Britain you have to go to school until you are 18. That would be another three years.

Even though I knew I was safe, I felt frightened all the time. I kept thinking about my family and all the things that had happened to me, especially about my village burning down and being in the jail in Libya. I dreamed of being back with my grandfather, sitting at his knee, hearing his wonderful stories about peace and different people, eating dates in the shade of a tree. But the dreams turned into nightmares.

I was afraid to sleep, so I was always exhausted. The headaches from Libya were getting worse and sometimes went on for days. The dreams had started coming in the daytime when I was awake. It's like they were happening on a television screen in my mind, my village burning, the bodies of my family, the dead bodies covered in flies on the streets of Libya, the torturers in the prison, being in the bin as it lifted into the air.

Throughout that time, my life was very busy with appointments. There was no time to lie on my bed and keep still and stop my head aching. As well as school, I was having extra English lessons, which felt pointless because I just couldn't seem to learn English. I could speak Arabic, Zaghawa and some Italian and French. But I couldn't manage English, and there were so many other things to learn that are all in English. How to cross roads, how to queue for things, how to order food in a café, how to go to the till at the supermarket, how people pass each other in the street.

There was strange food, cold weather, traffic lights. It was overwhelming. When you are homeless, all you think about is what you are going to eat and how you will keep the weather from you. You are alone – in a bush, on a bench, in the back of a church. You are quiet. Now everything was noise.

I also had to attend regular appointments with Chris, my social worker. Chris interviewed me about every part of my life for something called an Age Assessment. When you are a young asylum seeker like me and you have no documents or identification, one of the first things you have to do is to have your age confirmed and your needs assessed by social workers.

Chris explained that the Age Assessment was to confirm my age and that to get the right support for me, he needed to find out as much about my experiences as possible.

Chris said there was no question that I was a child. He said there was no doubt in his mind that I was 15, and that his assessment would secure my age with the Home Office because they would have to accept his decision. The Age Assessment would be shared with the Home Office and would help them know that I was telling the truth about my story – all the things about Darfur, Chad, Libya, France and now here.

That was very difficult because I didn't want to remember what had happened to me in all those places, and I didn't want to have to talk about my journey. But Chris said we would only have to do this once, and then it would all be written down in one place.

"It will be your history, your official document," he said.

Some of the bits were very upsetting, like when my village burned down and when I was tortured. Chris found it upsetting too, I could tell.

I told him about one of the worst days of my life, when I was living in the bin in France. Afterwards, I went and stood in the road and I hoped a car would run me over, but instead a kind lady stopped and took me to the church. Chris wrote it all down. He was learning about all the places I had lived too and reading up about Sudan and Libya. We looked at maps together. I am good at map reading. In one of the houses in Libya, the family used to have a big map on the wall and I used to just stare at it every day and look at all the countries I had been in and the ones I knew nothing of. I used to wonder if any of those countries had no wars, and whether people lived quietly there, without hunger or bombs or guns.

Another appointment I had to go to was with the psychiatrist, who was also doing a report on me. This was another person I had to talk to with a translator, and another person to tell my story to. The psychiatrist was very interested in the dreams I have when I am awake, where I can see things that happened to me still happening. He was interested in all the nightmares I have and the fact I only sleep about three hours most nights. He said that I might have Post Traumatic Stress Disorder and told me there were some different treatments I could have. During this time, I also had to go to CAMHS, Children and Adolescent Mental Health Services, for counselling about my anxiety and panic attacks.

Chris told me that when he had finished the Age Assessment sessions and all the early part of settling me into England, he would have to hand me over to a different social worker because his job was only for the first few months after a young person arrived. I was very sad, and Chris said he would see if he could ask permission for us to remain friends after he handed over my case, but that would be unusual. I hoped he could persuade the authorities, but didn't expect he would be able to. I had lost one parental figure after another all of my life.

In the meantime, there was some good news at last. Chris said social services had decided to move me from my foster parents. They agreed my first placement hadn't gone well. Chris said it was hard to get a match right sometimes. I thought Lesley and Graham seemed sad but also relieved I was going. I hadn't been able to talk to them very much or eat anything while I'd been staying with them, and I'd lost even more weight. The new clothes they gave me were falling off me. I hadn't slept either. When I looked in the mirror in their bathroom, I could see that my skin looked pale, and there were dark circles under my eyes.

The bad news was that I had to go back to the hostel until I could get another placement. At least my English was a little bit better by now, but I didn't feel safe there. It was warmer than being on the streets, but there were other people there who weren't kind, and who were drunk or on drugs, and who would steal things from you. Sometimes the streets felt safer.

After a few days, Chris came and picked me up to go to my new family. I said goodbye to Lesley and Graham and thanked them. All the while that black dog was in the hallway staring at me, giving me bad thoughts. I was glad to be moving away from it, and I thought maybe my luck would change now with that dog out of my life. Maybe the terrible dreams would go too?

Sarah's house was completely different to Lesley and Graham. It immediately felt like being in a family. There was Sarah and her partner Jack, and another foster child called Ben who was older than me. He was 16. He was actually from England but his parents weren't able to look after him, so he lived with Sarah and Jack.

Ben was quite naughty. Right away, he told me the word for "hello" was "vagina". When I said it to Sarah, to see if he was joking, she was angry with me and then angry with Ben when she realised he had tricked me into saying it.

I thought Ben was quite funny. He told me straight away he was going to teach me about PlayStation and football, "the two best things in life". I'd never played proper football with rules, or any video game. The only thing I'd ever played were riding camels and horses when I was a child and running in races in my village. I'd never seen a PlayStation before either. Ben was playing a game where you had to shoot people and I didn't like that game. By that time, my head was hurting anyway, so I said I needed to go to bed.

Living at Sarah's was better than my first foster placement, but I was still struggling to settle into the UK. One of the biggest struggles was over food. Sarah cooked English food, but I didn't like it. I had spent years cooking for Libyan families, and wanted to cook my own food, but I didn't always have all the ingredients. When I saw Sarah had bought a bag of onions or tomatoes I would cook them all up and eat them. Like many refugees, it was heavily ingrained in me to eat whatever was in front of me in case I didn't eat again. This was difficult for Sarah, who would find my wardrobe stuffed with onions and garlic and tins of food. She would come home and want to make dinner only to find I'd already used all the vegetables to make my dinner.

"Where are all the bananas, Abdul?" she would ask me. "There were six bananas here this morning."

I explained that I had been very hungry and eaten all the bananas.

"Abdul, there are other people who live in this house!" Sarah said. "They might have wanted a banana. And in any case, you will be ill if you eat six bananas in one day."

The other thing was milk. If I saw milk in the fridge, I would drink it. I was always thirsty. Sarah said I had to leave some for the rest of the family.

"12 pints of milk in three days is too much, Abdul," she said. "You can drink one pint a day. I can't afford any more. And in any case, you should drink water. It's not healthy to drink so much milk."

I found it very frustrating because I only had a tiny bit of money to last the week, and if I spent it on milk and onions and bananas, I had almost nothing and had to walk to all my appointments.

Another time, Sarah found me cooking meat straight out of the freezer. "You have to thaw it properly, Abdul," she said. "You can make yourself ill." I didn't really understand all these rules. I was more worried about whether the meat was halal.

Sometimes Sarah had to call a translator on the phone so that he could explain to me about my eating habits.

One day she caught me putting 12 sugars in my coffee.

"Abdul, this is really bad for you," Sarah said.

I wanted to explain that when I lived on the streets or during the war in Libya, if you found sugar you just filled your cup with it. My body has cravings for sugar and salt, all the things it was deprived of for so many years. It doesn't know when I will have sugar again, and it is very hard to resist the compulsion. In my heart, I am always preparing to flee and walk hundreds of miles into a new life. For that I need sugar.

Another thing I found frustrating was that I was always trying to put a fire on at Sarah's house. They had a fireplace, and when there was wood, I always wanted to light it because I was cold. Once it was lit, I would take off my socks and put my feet right into the fire, like we had when we were children, and as I'd done when I lived on the streets and someone would light a fire. Sarah would say, "Abdul, Abdul, take your feet out of the fire. We all want to share the warmth. In England, we don't just take our socks off and put our feet in the fire."

A problem I always had with the family was that I couldn't tell when someone was joking. Sometimes they would say something was a joke that didn't seem like a joke to me, or other times I would think they were joking when they were very serious. It was very confusing trying to work out all these things above the voices in my head, and the different language and all the things going on.

I did slowly learn football and PlayStation though, and in time, Ben and I became good friends. He's in the army now, fighting for the UK in all the wars around the world.

One morning, Sarah shouted up to me that she was going to the gym and she was going to take Ben with her.

"Do you want to come, Abdul?"

I said yes, but then I realised afterwards that I didn't have any money. I didn't know what to say to Sarah – I was very embarrassed. So, I just sat on my bed, with my head aching.

I could hear the car running downstairs, but I still couldn't get up.

Eventually Ben came to find me.

"Come on, Abdul!" he said.

I was lost in my thoughts and couldn't speak to him.

In the end, Sarah came to find me.

"Is it the money, Abdul?" she asked.

I nodded.

"I'll pay for you," she said. "Just come on. You'll enjoy it."

I have always enjoyed exercise of any kind. When I was child, we didn't think of it as exercise – it was working really, running with the animals, or running errands between the grazing lands and home. In England, when I ran, I felt completely free. I felt as if I could be anywhere in the world, running barefoot through Africa or in the green fields and woodland around Swindon. After a few minutes of running, my mind would calm down and my headache would go, and I would be able to think clearly.

I started running on my own, but one time I found some other people running so I joined in. People looked at me a bit strangely in my jeans and T-shirt but then they saw that I could run very fast and so they liked running with me. They spoke to me in English, but I didn't understand what they were saying. It was funny, because we all set off at the same time around a big park, but they only went around one time and I went around three times. I could have gone around even more times, but I decided to stop.

I noticed they all had short trousers on, so the next week before I went to meet them, I borrowed Sarah's scissors from the drawer and cut my jeans down to be like shorts. I was getting a bit hot running in jeans, so it seemed a good idea. But then I didn't have any jeans, and it was winter, and I had to go around in shorts.

Sarah wasn't happy at all about me making my own shorts and asked Chris the social worker to speak to me about it. He said he would take me shopping and we could get some new jeans. He also said that the college had lots of sports courses and we could find out about some.

"We need to talk about budgeting your money, Abdul, so you can buy shorts if you need some," Chris said. "You are getting a small allowance from the government now."

"I don't understand money," I told him. "I've never ever had any in my life."

On 24 September 2012, I had an appointment in Cardiff with the Home Office. It was at the Immigration Centre on Newport Road, an important-looking red brick building. It was where they decided if they believed all the things I had said about my journey, and to see if I could get my Leave to Remain – the paperwork that meant I could stay in the UK and not be sent back to France, or Libya, or Chad or Darfur.

Chris met me at Swindon train station, and we caught the hour-long train to Cardiff. I was very nervous. What if they didn't believe my story?

I don't remember much about the interview itself, but my files record that I told them: "Thank you very much to the British government. In France I had nothing. The people here feed me, and I have clothes and accommodation. I feel human again now."

Quite soon after that interview, Chris told me the Home Office had granted me full refugee status. He explained that this meant I couldn't now be sent back to any other country. I could hardly believe that it was true. I was finally safe here in the UK.

Sarah took me to the Harbour Project for refugees behind St Luke's Church in Swindon. Set up in 2000 to help Kosovar Albanian refugees from the war in Kosovo, it is still helping hundreds of people in a town that is home to speakers of 132 languages. In 2012, when I first went there, there were refugees and asylum-seekers there from all kinds of different wars across the world – Kosovo, Eritrea, Iraq, Kurdistan. But even so, I didn't feel at home there at first. It reminded me of living in the bombed-out house in Tripoli and of living with other refugees in the park in France. I didn't trust new people.

I was introduced to some other refugees from Sudan, but they were from the north of the country, from the tribes who had murdered my whole family. They were enemies. I didn't want to speak to them. They used to tease me about my Libyan accent.

"Abdul, I thought you were from Sudan!" they would laugh. "Why do you talk like a Libyan?"

One of them used to tease me and say I wasn't a man.

"Abdul, why are you crying?" he would say. "You aren't Sudanese. Sudanese men are warriors, they don't cry like children."

They used to laugh at me for playing with the little children's toys at the centre. I had never ever had any toys in my life, and I was fascinated by things like teddy bears, dolls' houses, Lego and toy cash registers and telephones. I often used to play with them along with the little children until I was aware of people staring at me.

I could still never seem to eat enough at Sarah's house, and she was always trying to stop me from over-eating with my sweet tooth, so when I went to the Harbour Project, I used to fill myself up with sandwiches and biscuits.

Sometimes I would just sit on the floor, cramming biscuits into my mouth from the coffee table where they were laid out on a plate for visitors.

One day at the Harbour Project when I was stuffing several biscuits down at a time, an English lady came over to see me. She was small with red hair and a kind face. She was one of the volunteers at the project. She said something to me.

"He doesn't speak English," I heard someone say.

Someone told me in Arabic.

"She is telling you, leave some biscuits for everyone else."

I was really angry with the lady.

"I'm hungry," I told her in broken English. "I have nothing to eat."

The lady asked me my name.

"Abdul," I said.

"How old are you, Abdul?"

I shrugged angrily. "15."

There was something about the lady. I was angry with her, but I liked her. She had the green eyes my grandfather had once told me about. "In the future," he used to tell us, "you will meet the white people who have green eyes."

"My name is Iris," she told me, bringing me over some food and drink. "But everyone calls me Ira." She told me she was 52 years old.

I watched Ira talking to other people. Then she went to sit in an armchair. All I could think was how I wanted someone to tell me a story the way that my grandfather used to tell me stories under the tree.

I picked up a book. I didn't know what it said. It had beautiful pictures all over it of animals and trees. I took it to Ira and gave it to her. She looked at me.

"What's this, Abdul?" she said.

I nodded at the book.

"You want me to read to you?"

I nodded.

I sat next to Ira on the floor and she started reading to me. I had no idea what the story was about or what she was saying, but I just enjoyed listening to the words and looking at the pictures. I felt the most relaxed I had felt in a long time.

After that, I went to find Ira every time I went to the Harbour Project and asked her to read to me. We became friends.

On the morning of Christmas Eve, I was at the supermarket with Sarah and Ben. I had been in the UK for five months and was still very far from settling in. Christmas songs were blaring over the tannoy, reminding me how happy everyone else was, and everything was very bright in the supermarket, shelves covered in tinsel and the staff in Santa hats. Everyone was buying food for their Christmas dinner, and the supermarket was packed with shoppers. I hadn't slept all night and was feeling terrible. I had a bad headache. Sarah was getting fed up because I kept complaining and I wasn't helping her to fill the trolley.

We were going down one of the aisles looking for sugar, when we bumped into Ira.

"Hello Abdul," Ira said. "Happy Christmas!"

I mumbled hello.

"Aren't you going to introduce us?" Sarah said.

"This is Ira, from the Harbour Project," I said. My head was aching even more with the effort of dealing with talking to someone.

"Abdul's not having a very good day," Sarah said. "He hates the supermarket."

I could never cope with the supermarket's garish light and confusing shelves, but Christmas time was the worst of all.

"Well, if Abdul ever wants to come and visit me, he's very welcome," Ira said.

"You know what, I think that might do Abdul good," Sarah said. "He definitely needs cheering up."

Sarah took Ira's phone number and we carried on with the shopping. It was very stressful and busy in the supermarket and my head was banging. Suddenly, all the thousands of things inside it made me feel angry. Why should these people here have all these thousands and thousands of things while people in Africa only had a little piece of cloth with some chilis and bananas spread out on it? Why were people hungry on the streets of Libya when people here had a choice of 30 different types of bread? I stomped off angrily down the aisle, hating everyone in the supermarket.

Later that afternoon, I told Sarah I would like to go to Ira's. I was still angry and exhausted and I thought maybe Ira would read me a story so I could just fall asleep in a chair.

"It's Christmas Eve, Abdul," Sarah said.

"She invited me," I said.

Sarah rang Ira, and Ira said it was fine for me to come and spend Christmas Eve with her. Sarah called me a taxi and I went to Ira's house. She lived out in the countryside, in a place called Wootton Bassett. It was a village surrounded by fields with animals. That made me happy, because I love animals and my family were farmers.

Ira explained she was going to her daughter Rachel's house for a Christmas Eve meal. She had rung her daughter, who said I was very welcome to come too.

I wasn't very happy about going to Ira's daughter's because I was shy, and I didn't really know how to socialise with people. I only wanted to see Ira. But I went to Rachel's house and we ate a nice dinner together and then I went off to explore the house by myself, rather than have to talk to new people.

I went into one of the rooms at the back and saw a strange machine that looked like something I had seen people running on at the gym. It had a long rubber belt and two handles. I stepped onto it and held the handles, and then I pressed a couple of buttons to see what would happen. The machine started whirring and the belt started moving quite quickly. I had to walk very fast to keep up with it. I tried to turn it off, but it just went faster and faster and I couldn't stop it. I was having to run and run to keep from falling over.

Just when I thought I couldn't run any more, and sweat was pouring off my face, the door burst open and Ira and her daughter appeared. They ran into the room and switched off the machine. They were both laughing so much they started crying.

"Oh Abdul!" Ira said.

Her daughter Rachel was looking at the machine.

"That's a pretty good run you've done there, Abdul," she said.

I was very proud of my run, and once I'd learned how to run on the machine properly, I loved it. But I always preferred to run outside, with the wind in my face and the trees and the birds.

I ended up spending most of Christmas with Ira and her family. I was struggling at Sarah's. I was so tired, and the terrible dreams were now with me all night and all day. I couldn't get away from my thoughts. I felt angry all the time. Angry about the people who had killed my family, angry with the people who had tortured me.

The safer I felt, the angrier I felt, because I knew Yusuf wasn't safe. Yusuf was still somewhere on my journey – trapped in a refugee camp, in a jail somewhere, living in a bin. I didn't know where he was, but thoughts of him cold, hungry, frightened and alone, maybe in pain, tortured my every moment.

I felt so angry and so sad I found it very hard to talk to anyone. Sometimes I felt like destroying everything around me. I also used to hoard things. It's something lots of refugees do. I'd hide food in my room and become very possessive about little things like pens and clothing.

After that, social services said they were finding me a new foster family, as Sarah had only been a short-term placement. They said there weren't any placements nearby and I would need to go to somewhere called Bristol. They said there was a bigger Sudanese community there. But I was worried the people would be northern Sudanese again. I was Darfuri, and I didn't want to be with people connected to the people who had killed my family. I identified more as Libyan than north Sudanese.

The next time I was at the Harbour Project I spoke to Ira about going to Bristol. She was really upset.

"You can't go all the way to Bristol," she said. "You're finally settling in here in Swindon, making friendships, and getting on better at school. You'd have to start again if you went to Bristol."

I shook my head. I wasn't settling in.

"Where would you like to go, Abdul," Ira asked?

"I only like it here at the Harbour Project," I said.

A few days later, I was at the project when Ira came up to me.

"If you like, you can come and live with me?" she said. "I've spoken to social services. They said that you can stay with me as a 'connected person' while I do a fostering course, and then later on I could foster you, if you like?"

I couldn't believe it.

"You mean, I could live with you?" I said.

Ira laughed. "Well, yes. I've got a three-bedroom house and my kids have left home. I've got plenty of space. I'm planning to downsize, but I can get somewhere with space enough for you and me."

She said she'd spoken to her daughter and she said, "Mum, you've got to keep Abdul. He can be our brother."

I thought that was funny. Like I was something somebody would keep.

"If I live with you, will you read to me when I can't sleep, Ira?" I asked her.

Ira nodded.

"Will we be able to go for walks to see the animals?"

"Yes," Ira said.

"I'll come and live with you, Ira," I said.

"What have I done?" Ira laughed.

Chapter Twelve
Liddington

Ira tried very hard to teach me English. I've since found out that something about the deep trauma I experienced as a child has affected my ability to learn language. I used to get all my words very confused, and I still struggle even after so many English lessons. One big problem was with nouns. I just couldn't get the word for "cooker". The word that always came into my mind was "cucumber", which made Ira laugh. And I was always doing things wrong. One day I tried to wash up the kettle to help Ira, but I ended up washing the whole thing in the sink and breaking it because it was electric.

I knew I drove Ira a bit mad with my hoarding.

"I've bought you a TV and a lovely lamp, Abdul, and you couldn't care less about them," she said to me. "All you care about are flags and pens. Every time I open a drawer there's nothing but pens in it."

In Africa, pens are very precious, and I dreamed of owning a biro with a plastic casing and ink running through it. I couldn't understand why English people didn't value pens the way I did and just left them lying around. I pocketed them almost compulsively. Flags I loved for their colours and what they said about a country. I collected them and learned all the different flags of the world. I had come through so many countries that the flags of Chad, Libya, France, the United Kingdom and Sudan held special meaning for me.

Ira moved to a place called Liddington, a picturesque village in the countryside close to an old Bronze and Iron Age hill fort. From there I could roam around the patchwork of green fields and go on long walks. Up on the hill was a "Starfish" control bunker from World War II, where bonfires used to be lit to draw the fire of the Luftwaffe away from Swindon. I couldn't imagine England being at war.

If I couldn't sleep at night, Ira would sit with me all night long and talk to me, or we'd just go and walk in the dark with a torch until I was tired. A few times, the flashbacks were so bad that I got into a very bad state and I couldn't breathe, and Ira had to call an ambulance. But mostly she would just cuddle me until I felt better. Eventually the attacks would pass.

Ira knew how much animals would calm me down, so if I was in a bad state, she would walk with me to the alpaca farm at the end of the fields, or to see cows or sheep, or horses. As soon as I felt bad, I would say, "Ira, please, let's go and see the alpacas."

Sometimes I would jump into the field with the animals and let them come to me. I felt very peaceful when I was with them. One day we went to visit the stones at Avebury, and the sheep nearby had just lambed. I climbed into the field, and the lambs let me pick them up and play with them.

"Abdul, I've noticed something very special happens when you are with animals," Ira told me. "They are completely calm and so are you. They come to you. And if I try to come over to you, they try to push me away. It's a special gift to be like that around animals."

I explained to her that I had grown up with animals and we lived with them as part of our family. I started riding when I was two years old and spent all my early life as a herder, sleeping with the animals, tending them, taking them to graze. Animals just know you, and you know them. There is nothing complicated. When I'm with any animals, but especially horses, I feel like I am a boy again, back with my family in the countryside.

Ira said she had heard of something called "equine therapy" which could help people who had experienced trauma like I had. Traumatised people spend time with horses to make them feel better. I had started seeing someone at CAMHS, the NHS mental health service, but the appointments were only once a month, and Ira knew how much I was struggling. She said she would look into equine therapy and see if there was anything like that near to Liddington.

In the meantime, she bought me probably the best present I had ever had: the most beautiful kitten. She had a fluffy coat of white fur, a small black face and bright blue eyes, and her name was Maisie. She slept curled up in a little shoebox. I loved that cat, and she used to follow me everywhere. Ira said she was like my daemon.

When I went out walking, sometimes I used to get into trouble for going on people's land, because I never really understood why land belonged to people. Where I came from the land was just the land, and it was grazed by nomads. Ira was always telling me not to go down to the lake near where we lived because it was on land that belonged to Lord Joel Joffe, a famous lawyer who had defended Nelson Mandela. I liked it that he had grown up in Africa too.

I still used to go down to the lake because I liked it there, and I liked the gardens around the old stone manor house. I could easily get lost in them because they had so many hedges and beech and sequoia trees. There was a stream that led down to a tennis court and a summer house.

I used to sit by the lake for hours, looking for fish and watching the frogs and dragonflies. White lilies bloomed on giant lilypads, and the manor house was reflected in the still water with its patches of green algae. I know Lord Joffe saw me because sometimes I saw him watching me from the window, but he never told me to get off the land or complained about it. Maybe he was pleased to see someone from Africa too.

One time, when I was out in the countryside, I remembered being a child and making mud animals. I made some for Ira – an elephant, a rhino, a lion and a giraffe. She couldn't believe it when she saw them.

"These are so beautiful, Abdul," she said. "Where did you learn to do that?"

"We never had any toys when I was a child," I told her. "We used to make them in the fields, and then I used to make them with Yusuf in the dirt in the refugee camp. I used to do it all the time, mum."

Ira looked at me as if she was going to cry and I knew she didn't mind me calling her mum.

I told Ira I wanted to start going to the local mosque because although I still prayed regularly, I hadn't been to the mosque since I'd arrived in the UK and I still had a lot to thank God for in keeping me alive through my long journey. It was coming up to Ramadan, which was always a very important time to go. Ira said the nearest one was in Swindon and that she would take me there. The mosque was in a run-down area, so Ira said she would wait outside for me in the car and bring me home again in case of any trouble.

The mosque was an old red-brick building that Ira said was probably once a church. Inside it had wooden beams and a thick red and gold carpet on which I prostrated myself, thanking God for bringing me safely to Swindon.

I was there a very long time praying, and when I finally came out two hours later, Ira was talking to a police officer. I was frightened.

"Is this the boy you are waiting for?" the policeman asked.

Ira nodded.

"Next time, don't loiter here," the policeman said. He allowed himself a smile. "And, if you do, keep your door locked."

Ira explained the mosque was in something called a "red-light area", where men came to look for ladies selling sex. The policeman had stopped Ira because he thought she was one of those ladies.

"A man tapped on my window and asked me 'are you looking for business'," Ira laughed.

"That was bad enough, but then the police tried to arrest me for soliciting. I told them, 'I'm a 51-year-old woman playing Candy Crush on my phone. I'd be the one paying them'."

Ira had told the police she was actually waiting for her son, who was at the mosque. Seeing as she was a white woman, they had found this excuse very dubious.

"Pull the other one," they told her.

"At least we've been to the mosque now," Ira said.

"We have to go every day in Ramadan, mum," I told her.

"Bloody hell, Abdul," she said.

People were very kind in Liddington. Everyone I met used to say, "Hi, Abdul." They all seemed to know who I was. I suppose I stood out in that very English village. There weren't many people with black skin.

I used to see our neighbour, Vince, running past Ira's house all the time. One day, he came and knocked on our door as he went past.

"I hear you're a runner, Abdul," he said.

I said I was.

"Why don't you come with me today? I could use the company."

I said yes because I loved running. We went running and did quite a few miles. Vince couldn't believe it. He was the one who got tired. I wasn't even tired when we got back.

"We need to get Abdul doing some competitions, Ira," he said.

I started running a lot after that. It cleared my head and helped me with sleeping. I went on to win the Swindon, Cheddar and Eton half marathons.

One day, Vince asked if I'd like to come up in his light aircraft. I had seen him flying overhead and wondered what it would be like to be up in the air in a tiny plane and what the world would look like. I thought, "Well, that's one thing you've never done before in your crazy life, Abdul."

When the plane took off, I was terrified. The land just started rushing away and the plane made a huge noise. Suddenly we were up in the air and down below the buildings and trees were turning into toys. I felt sick in my stomach. But after we had been in the air a few moments, I loved it. I felt free.

After that, Vince often asked me to go up in the plane, and I always went with him.

"Come flying, Abdul," he would say. "Or, come running, Abdul." It was good to have a friend in my new neighbourhood.

That year was my first real Christmas. The previous year I had just been visiting. But now I was one of the family. I spent a long time saving up my money to buy a present for Ira and wondering what to get. Ira was cross with me because she'd had a £50 non-attendance penalty from college, because I hated going there so much. I wanted to make it up to her.

We spent a lovely afternoon stringing up lights on the trees outside Ira's house, climbing on a ladder. When it finally got dark and we switched them on they looked magical. I could see them from my bedroom window when I couldn't sleep at night.

I loved working in the garden, planting things and nurturing them, watching them grow under the sun and the rain. But I hated the cold and found it harder to go outside in winter. I just wanted to stay curled up on Ira's sofa or spend long days in bed with Maisie the cat. Ira had got Maisie for me when I started my treatment for Post-Traumatic Stress Disorder. It meant that when I felt bad I didn't have to go out in the cold to see the llamas and the alpacas, I could just sit with Maisie. Just stroking her soft fur made me feel calmer. I trusted her in a way I still struggled to with humans, and I felt she understood me. I've always believed humans are meant to be with animals.

I loved every minute of that Christmas. I discovered it was a time when English people spend a lot of time staying in and watching films on the television. My favourite was *Lawrence of Arabia*. Lawrence rode through the sand on camels like my family used to do, and I loved the scenes of the burning desert at sundown, where you could see the air shimmering. I could imagine myself riding through the desert with my head wrapped in a turban, into new adventures. I couldn't believe the film had been made so many years ago.

In the end I bought Ira some perfume and a slow cooker because I knew she really wanted one. Ira is a really great cook and I love her dinners. She's not as good a cook as me, of course.

Another friend I had in the village was a retired teacher who lived in a wonderful thatched cottage with the most beautiful garden I had ever seen. I called her Sister Barbara.

One day, she saw me walking through her garden admiring the colours of her flowers and sniffing the petals. I had never smelled such beautiful flowers.

"Excuse me," she said. "Have I met you before?"

I started to apologise.

"I'm sorry," I said. "You have a lovely garden… and a lovely house."

She smiled at me.

"Well, would you perhaps like to come in?"

The old cottage was full of shelves packed with amazing books of all shapes and sizes. I had never seen so many, even in a library. Sister Barbara saw me looking at them.

"Do you like books, Abdul?" she said.

"I love stories," I said. "But I can't read." I shrugged. "I'm trying to learn, but it's not going very well."

Sister Barbara asked me to choose a book and then we sat down on her sofa and read it together. I still always loved to be read to, and she had a lovely way of reading.

After that I used to call in if I was passing that way. Sister Barbara would welcome me with a big wave at the window. Sometimes we would sit and have tea and cake together, and she would ask me all about the places I had been to and what they were like.

On her shelves, Sister Barbara had huge books of maps, which I loved to look at. We would often look at the map of Africa together and I would tell her all the countries I had walked through and trace the journey on the map with my finger. I could soon recognise all the towns and cities I had come through. Seeing them on the printed page seemed to make the eight years of my journey real, as it if it had been written down in drawings.

Sister Barbara taught me about gardening and showed me how to mow the lawn and weed the flowerbeds. She showed me how to trim the hedges and cut back plants that were growing too unruly. Then she said she would pay me a little bit of money to do the gardening for her as she was getting older.

She said I could pick the strawberries in her garden any time and eat them. I had recently learned to cycle, so in the summer holidays I would go over every day weeding and mowing and watering the plants and eating the strawberries. Her garden had huge flowerbeds with blue, purple, white and pink flowers, and there was always weeding to do.

One day when I got to the house, I knocked on the door as usual, but Sister Barbara wasn't in. I cycled home again, and then came back later. She still wasn't in. Something felt strange because the garage door had been left open.

I cycled home again and found Ira.

"Mum, something is wrong at Sister Barbara's," I said.

Ira came to the house with me, but we couldn't find anyone in.

"Maybe Sister Barbara has gone on holiday," Ira said.

I was still worried. I thought Sister Barbara would have told me if she were going away, and why would she leave the garage door open?

Ira thought that her daughter might have been in keeping an eye on the house while she was away.

Four days later, the phone rang with the news that Sister Barbara had passed away. I was extremely upset to think she might have been lying there when I knocked at the door. Ira was upset too.

Sister Barbara's daughter told us that when the paramedics went in, there was a large Atlas on the coffee table. Its pages were open on a map of my country, Sudan.

"She must have been looking forward to Abdul's visit," she said.

I didn't know what to do after that. I was very, very, angry, and upset. Sister Barbara was yet another person taken away from me. Another friend lost. It made me remember the pain of losing my parents, and Yusuf, and Aboud and my grandfather all over again. Why did God want me to be alone in the world?

Every day for the rest of that summer, I cycled to Sister Barbara's house and did her weeding. I didn't know what else to do.

Around that time, I received a letter from a boy I'd met in Libya when we were living in the bombed-out house in Tripoli. I barely remembered him, or anything from that time, but it felt good to have some connection to the past. Khaled said he was now in England. He had been looking for me and anyone else from Libya through the Red Cross family-tracing service. Ira had helped me register onto the scheme in the hope of finding Yusuf. It meant if he ever turned up at a refugee camp or a border and was registered, the computer would find a match.

I spoke to Khaled a few times on the phone, and he came to visit. Seeing someone from my past was good and bad. It was wonderful to be with someone who understood some of my journey, but it brought things back. And Khaled was very sad and angry. Ira said I was different when I was with him. Withdrawn, and angry myself sometimes. Khaled was very traumatised by some of the things he'd seen in Libya. He constantly spoke of getting on a boat to Calais to try to find his family and friends. He was convinced they were there.

"You need to come with me," he said. "We will look for my family and we will look for Yusuf."

I was very unsure.

"But why would we go the other way, Khaled?" I said. "We are safe here. Why would we want to cross the channel the other way? Anyway, we don't have passports."

"What about Yusuf?" Khaled said. "Are you just going to abandon him?"

That winter, the flashbacks got worse again. I hated the cold and dark. I kept seeing the Janjaweed approaching again and again, in a trail of fire. I was still seeing CAMHS, and Ira had heard about a treatment called EMDR – Eye Movement Desensitisation and Reprocessing – which she managed to get a charity to fund for me. It helped to control the panic attacks and to stop the flashbacks taking over my life. But I was so afraid of my dreams that I barely slept, and my memories could wash over me at any time. I spent more and more time out running, cycling or walking with Ira.

Ira's daughter Georgina, who everyone calls George but I used to call Yellow Sister because of her hair, said I needed to spend more time with people my own age, and took me to London's Notting Hill Carnival. I loved the music and being surrounded by so many people that looked like me, but I struggled with the crowds and was shocked to see so many women drinking. In Africa, you never see women drinking. At Notting Hill Carnival a lot of women were very drunk.

One day we were walking in the cold and Ira said she was worried about me because I was so sad.

"Abdul," she said, "one day when you are older you will get your British passport and you can go back to Sudan, find your village and say, this is my land."

I was filled with rage. Even Ira wanted to send me home now. She was supposed to be my mum, but she wanted me to go back to Sudan. I started kicking the fence, over and over. When Ira tried to stop me, I ran home.

Later, she came to talk to me in my room.

"Abdul, I spoke to one of your friends and told them what I said to you. I said I didn't know why I had made you so angry."

I was still too angry to speak.

"I wasn't telling you to go back home. Your home is here now. But I was trying to say to you that one day you will be able to go back if you want to, and see where you came from."

Worse was to come. On 8 February 2015, I turned 18 years old. That was the end of the care system for me. Ira had other children who needed her care, and I was no longer her responsibility. I took this news very hard. Chris hadn't been my social worker for some time by then either. He had managed to get permission for us to keep in touch, but he had moved to a different job in another city and so it was difficult for us to see each other. I started to feel as if I was alone again.

I moved back into temporary accommodation later that year, setting down the few things I owned in a rucksack and a couple of plastic bags.

Ira had told me she would always be my mum whatever happened, but I knew that other young people needed her help now. Moving out felt like being homeless again, even though I had a roof over my head. I was no longer part of a family, and was completely alone. I still didn't understand how England worked, and I was still finding English very difficult, especially when I felt anxious.

To make things worse, I was moved back into the accommodation I had started in when I first arrived in the UK. It reminded me of how I felt in those days – frightened, alone, unable to eat and barely functioning as a human being. The flat on County Road in Swindon had a musty smell and the windows were filthy. When I made the bed, clouds of dust came out of it, and when I woke up the next day with my body covered in red welts, I realised the mattress was full of bed bugs. The other people in the hostel were a collection of single men with drug and alcohol problems. They frightened me with their drunken shouting. Men would bang on my door at night.

My lock was frequently broken, and food and cash stolen from my room.

An older man started bullying me. He used to break into my room when I wasn't there and steal food and money. The flashbacks were very bad, and I couldn't seem to cope with anything.

Letters were piling up for me in the hallway. I opened the top one, which said: "You have not paid your service charge for six weeks and are now at risk of eviction." I threw it in the bin.

The police were often called, and every time I heard their sirens or saw them pass in their uniforms, I felt utter terror, expecting them to take me to prison. Since Libya, I had been terrified of anyone in military or service uniforms. They came so often I began to think they were watching me all the time. When I witnessed an assault and had to give evidence to the police, I was so frightened at the police station it was as if I had been the one to commit the crime.

I no longer felt safe, and my mental health began to deteriorate badly. My sleep had been a little better in the final months at Ira's, but now I completely stopped sleeping again, just finally crashing for two or three hours when dawn broke and I felt safer knowing the black night was over. Worse, the intrusive thoughts I had about the burned-out faces and bodies of my parents and my torturers in Libya came back. There was no escaping them, awake or asleep. At Ira's I had learned to live with these images, but now they were paralysing. I stopped going to college or leaving my room except to scavenge for food. I spent the days obsessively washing my hands, my clothing and my bed, trying to get the place clean.

After a particularly bad night when the men were knocking on my door, I decided I was safer on the streets than in that place at night. I found a park bench in the centre of town and began sleeping there in the daytime and moving about in the shadows at night. I'd lived like that before in France, and the two experiences began to join up in my mind. It was as if all that time living happily and safely at Ira's had never happened.

It felt like everything I had done – my whole journey from Sudan to here, over all those many years – had been completely pointless. I still had no family. My parents were still dead. I was still someone with no home and no tribe and no belongings. I didn't belong to anyone or anywhere.

That November, I started crossing dangerous roads on purpose, and standing in the middle of them to see what would happen. I didn't run in front of cars, but I didn't avoid them either. I just stood in the road to see if I would be lucky and die, or unlucky and continue living. Usually the cars swerved and hooted. One time somebody called the police, but they couldn't catch me.

Calais Jungle refugee camp, France

Chapter Thirteen
Calais

Khaled had rung me repeatedly over the summer about his plans to go to Calais. Today, we were finally going with another boy from the mosque, Tanweer. I didn't tell Ira because I knew she would be angry. I was living on my own, I was 18 years old – a man now.

I had saved up some money to get a bus to London, and Khaled said he'd got our tickets from there. He had some sort of job washing cars and had been saving up. We took a coach from London to Dover. Khaled was in a strange mood and seemed angry. He had become very religious recently, growing a beard and praying all the time. My religion remained very important to me – I kept halal, and I prayed five times a day, but Khaled seemed to be talking in a different way.

I was already worried that people seemed to be treating me differently since the terror attacks at the

Bataclan in Paris that November. It felt like every time I turned on the news there was something bad about Muslims and what they had done. I had no way of telling people that I would never, ever get involved in something like that. That my parents had been killed by terrorists, and my village burned by Arab Muslim horsemen. That I hated war and abhorred violence and had gone to jail in Libya and been tortured rather than fight for Colonel Gaddafi.

When we got to the check-in for the ferry, I was worried I wouldn't be let on with my ID card, but Khaled produced three ID cards in different names for him, me and Tanweer. I was frightened, but the immigration official barely looked at them, waving us through.

The wintry sea was very rough. The journey reminded me of the boat I had taken from Libya to France, except this time it was the white cliffs of the English coast that were slowly disappearing from view. As we lost sight of them, I began to panic, and then the French coast came into clear view.

I was still confused about why we were travelling in the wrong direction, back to France, the country that had left me destitute. Khaled said he had a plan and I should stop worrying. He had an idea where we could look for his and Tanweer's families, and might find Yusuf.

When we arrived at Calais, I was glad to be off the rocking boat. My legs were still trembling afterwards, and I still felt sick. I didn't dare to hope we would find Yusuf, but I knew I had to try everything I possibly could.

Khaled's friends picked us up in Calais in a battered car, and drove us to the main camp. This was Jungle II – the second camp built by migrants and supported by charities since the first one had been demolished. A day centre run by volunteers was offering one meal a day, water taps and showers. But it was quickly clear that the centre was overrun and conditions in the camp were desperate. It was bitterly cold already in November, and the smell of sewage hung like a blanket in the air. The people were not even afforded the security of a refugee camp. It was an illegal camp, and the police regularly raided it and dispersed its inhabitants, giving the place an air of anxiety and meaning the structures were poorly built.

I could immediately see that Sudanese people made up a huge number of the migrants trapped in that hell. Sudanese and Afghans seemed to account for an easy majority of those coming and going from the day centre.

As far as the eye could see there were tents, or sometimes just pieces of filthy canvas strung out on wire or rope or across wooden pallets. Some people had tried to create wooden structures to better keep out the wind, rain and mud, and just like in Chad there were improvised cafes and barbers, and bitterly ironic signs saying "Five-Star Hotel!"

Between the tents were little firepits made with rocks, with kettles and pans. There was lots of litter trodden into the dirt, and there were groups of young men with tired eyes just sitting and staring, waiting for nightfall to try their luck on the trains and lorries again. Some had injured arms or legs from the barbed wire protecting the container port and the railways.

These people, Khaled explained, kicking through empty tear gas canisters, were the bottom of the migrant food chain. Migrants with more money and better contacts got on lorries far south of Calais, avoiding the port altogether.

I didn't know what Yusuf looked like now. He would be 16 years old. A young man. But that didn't stop me seeing him in every Sudanese migrant crouched over a fire or carrying wood or huddled inside a makeshift tent. I started going from tent to tent asking, "Has anyone seen Yusuf Musa Adam, a boy from Darfur? Are there any Darfuris here? Any Zaghawa? Any African migrants from Libya?"

The people I spoke to looked exhausted and hollowed out, the way I looked when I was on the streets in France. I didn't look much better now. I hadn't been taking care of myself since I left Ira's. I was too thin, and my hair was unkempt, and my clothes were filthy. I had stopped sleeping again.

"There are some people from Libya over there," a man in a smart brown *shalwar kameez* told me. "Good luck."

I chatted to the Libyans, who were kind and admired my Libyan accent.

"Hear him speak! He's like a Libyan, not a Zaghawa?"

But they knew nothing about Yusuf. A few people asked me for money or food, but half-heartedly. They could see I was as destitute as them.

Jungle II had been up for eight months, and after being there a long time, some people had made homes in their tents even though they were being faced again with eviction. A kind South Sudanese Dinka lady invited me to drink some tea with her inside a little tent that had a neatly made bed on the floor and a little lantern. A picture of Jesus was tacked up on the wall.

"You are safe in England," she said. "Don't come here. The authorities will catch you and then you might never get back to England again."

"I don't have a choice, I have to find Yusuf," I said. "Until I find him, I will never be happy, and I will never be safe. Every day that I am in a warm bed and Yusuf is out in the cold and the rain somewhere, I feel I am in the cold and the rain."

The lady brought out a little piece of wood and started chopping chillies on it with a knife that had no handle. She invited me to stay for dinner – some tomatoes and chillies and a bit of rice. While we were chatting, her daughter came back, pushing a shopping trolley full of heavy water containers, and I saw she was pregnant.

"There are thousands and thousands of people here, Abdul," the lady said. "Not just here, but all along the border of northern France, and along other European borders. You won't find Yusuf here. He must find you."

It was getting dark, I'd lost Khaled, and the lady asked if I had anywhere to sleep.

"It's best not to be out after dark," she said.

"Thank you," I said. "But I need to keep looking for Yusuf."

As the sun was setting over the sprawling camp made of rubbish and tarpaulin, I decided to go from tent to tent for as many hours as I could. Families would be together then, and it would be easier to speak to people.

"Has anyone seen Yusuf Musa Adam?" I called. "Any Darfuri Sudanese? Any Zaghawa? Anyone from Libya?" I tried in all the languages I could remember – Zaghawa, Arabic, Italian, French and English.

Many people called me over and tried to help me. Everyone in the Jungle has lost someone, often many people, and they understand the desperation you feel when your sibling is lost. People were so kind, that I almost began to feel as if I should just stay in the camp, among people who understood me, and where I might one day find Yusuf. I felt more at home there than in the hostel in Swindon. While I was in the camp, the way I felt inside matched my surroundings.

After I had been going from tent to tent for a few hours, I reached the edge of the camp. I paused for a moment, wondering which path to take next. Then I heard the sound of lots of different voices shouting, getting nearer and nearer. I had no torch, and couldn't see far into the blackness, but suddenly I became aware of dozens of men running towards me, arms flailing, kicking up the mud with their shoes.

"Run!" they shouted. "Run for it! *Allez! Dépêche toi!*"

I didn't know where to run to. There were men running behind them in black uniforms carrying torches, with dogs. When they reached me, I started running, but too late. One of the men grabbed me and pinned me to the ground. Another man shone a flashlight in my face.

"I've caught one," he shouted in French. "Come on, my young friend."

The men took me to a van. In the torchlight I could see they were gendarmes – they had "POLICE" on their backs. They drove me to the police station in Calais, where I was searched.

The policeman looked bored.

"Why were you trying to get on the train?" he asked me.

"I wasn't," I said. "I'm British. I live in England. I am here to look for my brother."

He threw the ID card Khaled had got me down onto the table.

"This is fake. It's not you. So no, you are not British."

"I promise you, I am British," I said. "I have five years Leave to Remain in the UK. This is not my ID card. I don't know why I have it."

"Where's your ID card, then?" the policeman said.

"Ask the British police, they will find me. My name is Abdul Musa Adam. Date of birth 08.02.97. I am a refugee from Sudan, and the UK has given me refugee status."

"Why on earth would you be so stupid as to be here, then?"

I spent the night in the cold cells and in the morning, I was turned over to the custody of the British police. I explained everything to them and said I didn't care what happened to me now. I only wanted to find my brother Yusuf. They checked with immigration and rang Ira, who explained I had PTSD and other problems and didn't always act very logically. They let me speak to Ira, who said she was worried sick and that I was in serious trouble.

The nice policeman got the boat back with me to Dover and was kind when I vomited the whole way back again, bringing me some water. He said he didn't know what had happened to Khaled. Maybe he was still in the camp. His phone was no longer working but I texted it anyway.

I wrote: *Do not contact me again, Khaled, you are a bad friend. Now I might be sent back to Sudan because of your crazy ideas.*

After being in the Jungle, I couldn't sleep for images of Yusuf. I imagined him in one of those cold, draughty tents with a mud floor and newspaper for a carpet, trying to cook scraps of food on a windy fire. I imagined him trapped on the barbed wire, and running from the police, or suffocating in the back of a smugglers' lorry. I tried to remember the Dinka lady's words, how she'd said he might not even be there.

The police visited me again in Swindon and spoke to me about the incident. They were going to take no further action against me given everything I had been through.

"But if you are ever caught doing anything like this again, you will be in extremely serious trouble," the officer said. "You have had a very lucky escape, Abdul."

One cold December morning, I decided that I was never going to find my brother and things were never going to get better for me, and I just needed to call an end to it all. I couldn't take the thoughts anymore. I needed to make them stop, and I couldn't escape them in my sleep, by watching TV or even by running. I decided the only way to make my brain stop remembering was to switch myself off. Stop the dreams. Stop the flashbacks. Stop the thinking.

I wanted to be with my parents, and my sisters, and Aboud, and the other people from my village. I didn't want to be alone in a strange land anymore, thinking about everyone I had lost, and all the things that had been done to me.

My parents had died in a fire, and I decided that was how I would die. I went to my room in the hostel and put some paper and bits of wood I had collected into the metal wastepaper bin to start the fire off, but I couldn't get a fire going. I didn't want to give up, so I walked a mile or so to the nearest petrol station and picked up a can of petrol. It was quite heavy when I took it to the till.

"Do you have ID?" the cashier asked.

I wondered if I looked strange or mad. He was looking at me with a worried expression.

I didn't have any ID with me.

"I'm 18," I said.

"Well that's as may be, but I need to see ID, I'm afraid," the cashier said.

I was angry and left the shop. When I got back, I tried to make the fire again in the bin and it caught a bit more alight, but it set all the fire alarms off. The fire brigade arrived before more than a few things had caught fire. The police arrived at the same time.

I tried to run away because I was terrified, but a nice policewoman spoke to me.

"What's your name?"

"Abdul," I whispered.

"What were you trying to do?" the policewoman asked me.

"To set fire to myself," I told her. "I hoped to die."

She said she would call social services, and they would look after me.

"It's okay, Abdul," she said.

The next day Ira came to find me.

"I've found some equine therapy for you," she said. "It's the one I was telling you about – where you spend time with horses. You can go under a care leavers' programme. You need more support, Abdul."

She showed me a website about "Animal-Assisted Intervention". Greatwood was a place where they took retired racehorses and rescue horses and matched them with people who could benefit from them.

I told Ira I didn't want to go. I was very tired. I hated meeting new people. It was in the countryside near Marlborough, and I was going to have to get the bus for an hour to get there and I always got lost because my English was bad. It was freezing cold and the days were short and the dark made my moods even worse.

Ira told me, "Abdul, you can't go on like this. You are going."

Chapter Fourteen
Greatwood

The first day I went to Greatwood, in August 2015, I was a very anxious 18-year-old. I had hardly slept the night before. PTSD had a grip on me, meaning that even though I had previously crossed continents and national borders in traffickers' buses and crossed raging seas, now even taking public transport filled me with deep anxiety. The bus took over an hour from Swindon. I was in a frail mental state and the thought of meeting new people was exhausting. Several times I thought about just going home again.

Greatwood charity is set in acres of green land on the North Wessex Downs near the town of Marlborough. The bus dropped me at the nearest main road and then I started walking through the countryside in the warm morning sunshine, following the directions Ira had given me. Eventually I saw the sign for "Greatwood" and turned down a country lane, with a wide hedge on one side, and a large green paddock on the other. It was a beautiful setting. It had been a cool and wet summer and the fields and trees were thick with flowers, insects and bird life. After the weeks I'd spent in Swindon, I was glad to be back in the fields, with the smell of flowers, farmyard and nearby animals.

In the paddock, a dozen or so huge brown horses were standing silently still, grazing in groups and trying to ignore some more spirited horses chasing each other around the green field. I stopped for a while and leaned on the fence to look at them. I resisted the urge to climb over and talk to them because I knew I was late to register.

At the end of the drive I found a warm reception building busy with people in wellies and riding boots, and dogs of varying sizes. A sign said: "People helping horses. Horses helping people." There were a few people milling about. I was immediately nervous and thought again about going home. But something about the horses I had watched on the way in made me want to stay.

"You must be Abdul," a silver-haired lady said to me. She was wearing a purple T-shirt with the Greatwood crest on it. Her name was Helen, she said.

I nodded. I didn't really speak at all during that time unless something was very important.

"Well, it's lovely to meet you, Abdul," Helen said. "Come with me."

Greatwood was founded by Helen Yeadon and her husband Michael, who had been rescuing horses together since 1998. Former racehorse owners, riders and breeders, they had long been worried about what happened to horses once they could no longer race. The horses they had first rescued had been abandoned, maltreated, even sold in card games. But Greatwood was born when a friend asked them if they could help a little girl who had become so withdrawn she had stopped speaking.

Helen and Michael had just rescued a horse that was in a very bad way. To their astonishment, the girl and horse were able to help each other in a remarkable way, building the self-esteem of each other through the bond they made.

All I knew at that time was that this was a place where I could spend the day with horses. Helen said we could look around Greatwood, but all I wanted to do was to get into the fields. For a while, we walked around the grounds, looking at the chicken coop, the raised vegetable beds and the horses running in the paddock. Fields stretched into the distance beyond, and the distant shadows of more horses were dotted about on the horizon.

Helen told me there were 38 retired and rescued horses at Greatwood. There were also 25 hens, she said, as she introduced me to the cockerels with their black feathers and red coxcombs running happily about the place.

"This one is called Peter Andre," she told me.

Another cockerel rushed past us busily, on his way somewhere.

"And this one," Helen said, "is called Lunch."

Of all the animals at Greatwood, I immediately fell in love with the ponies. We had had ponies growing up – and there is even a breed called the Darfur pony. The ponies loved me too. They kept nuzzling into me and nipping my arms. I couldn't stop hugging them.

After a while, Helen took me for a long walk to the back fields, where we could see some older, dignified, magnificent animals standing, or moving slowly between a pool of water and short, green grass. These ex-racehorses were tall, strong beasts, weighing up to 2,000 lb, whose hooves or powerful shoulders could crush you in a moment. But I knew they wouldn't hurt me. These Thoroughbred horses were the closest I'd ever seen in England to the horses I remembered from my childhood in Darfur.

Helen explained that they rehomed many of the horses that came to Greatwood, but that this sanctuary field was for racehorses that would never be rehomed because they had been neglected too long or had a difficult temperament or were just too old.

"This is their last chance at the O.K. Corral," Helen said. I nodded even though I didn't know what that meant.

"Want to go in?"

I nodded.

Helen opened the gate and I walked towards a group of horses, speaking quietly under my breath in Arabic. A horse came towards me, nodding his head, and pushing into me. He was ten times my strength, and far taller. His shove to my shoulder almost knocked me over. I caught his head with my hand and scratched his neck, pulling him towards me. The familiar scent of the horse took me back, way beyond any recent experience, to the scrubland of Darfur. As I hugged him, and he breathed into my neck, I felt I was suddenly home, as if my parents weren't far away and I was just out in the fields. I felt my shoulders relax and a great weight lifted off me for a few moments.

As I held onto him, I wondered about his journey to Greatwood. He had once been a cossetted racehorse worth thousands of pounds and fed only the best hay, sleeping only in the best bedding, ridden and washed and groomed on a daily basis. Yet his life had been turned upside down by some event. Had he lost races, been injured, been sold to a bad owner? How had he ended up searching, like me, for a safe home?

The earliest recorded mention of horse therapy is the writings of Hippocrates in Ancient Greece. In the 19th century, German doctors used to advise horse-riding to reduce attacks of hysteria. Horses are herd animals, highly attuned to respond to the fear or excitement in others in the group. They mirror and respond without humans having to explain things to them. Thoroughbred horses, perhaps most of all, know how you are feeling from the moment you join their herd. They never judge who you are now or what you have done in your life. They don't care if you are from Sudan or England or Libya. They can hear a human heartbeat much better than a stethoscope and their own hearts even begin to beat with yours, gradually slowing a human's agitated heart to a gentler pace.

Over the next five days, I worked on the "Get Going Programme" at Greatwood, an intensive programme where I learned to take care of horses. I loved that every moment of the programme my mind was busy thinking about the horse and all the things I had to do, instead of thinking about the past, and I enjoyed the companionable silence of being with the horses. It's a quiet that is never really quiet because you and the horse are communicating all the time.

I got to know Helen and Michael, and I was looked after a lot of the time by Sasha Thorbek. There were a few other people on the course as well, who had their own troubles but weren't angry like the people at the hostel. Being around horses seemed to help them too.

On the first day, Sasha came to see how I was getting on.

"I can see you are good with horses, Abdul," she said. "Have you worked with horses before?"

I wanted to explain to her about the horses my family had owned in Darfur, and how I had taken care of them and ridden them from the age of two and how my father and sister were the best riders in our group of nomads. But I still wasn't confident enough in English and, in any case, I was too shy.

Greatwood is spread out across old farm buildings, and many of the horses live in an old milking parlour that Michael and Helen renovated from derelict years ago. Over the next five days, I learned the points of a horse – dozens of them, from the forelock to the withers, and the gaskin to the coronet. I learned the difference between the cannon and the fetlock and the muzzle and the bridge of the nose. I learned the difference between mucking out, where you re-do the horse's whole bed with fresh wood shavings, and skipping out, where you just clean up the horse's droppings.

I rode a mechanical racehorse and visited a racing yard, which I loved. There were so many huge and beautiful horses there, but it was so calm and ordered. Every person there knew exactly what they were doing and when to do it. I learned that Thoroughbreds born in the northern hemisphere all have the same birthday of January 1 each year, while those born in the southern hemisphere have an official birthday of August 1.

At the end of the five days, I was stunned to find I had passed the first test I had ever passed in my life: the 1st4Sport Entry Level 2 Award in Assisting with Basic Care of Horses. Helen sat me down and said they'd like to offer me the chance to do some longer training with them – a programme called Horse Power.

"It will be more challenging than the last course, Abdul," she said. "You'll have to work very hard, but I know you can do it."

It was hard for me to get from the hostel in Swindon to Greatwood each day, so Sasha kindly suggested she would pick me up each day from outside Lloyds Bank in Marlborough. I had to get the bus from Swindon to Marlborough every day at 8.30am, and then Sasha picked me up at 9.15 for a 9.30 start at Greatwood.

When I arrived each day, I was given a cup of tea and a nice hot breakfast of some toast and eggs. I think they realised I wasn't eating very much otherwise, because of having no money and often coming straight from sleeping in the shopping precinct.

I was assigned to a tutor called Jane, who was experienced in therapeutic work. In the morning I would do classroom work, mainly literacy and maths. In the afternoon, it was the work I loved: practical work with the horses. Sometimes if I had had a bit of sleep, I would find the day easier. Other days, it was a huge strain just for me to get there, and I found the morning classes too much.

Some of the horses at Greatwood are famous winners, like Deano's Beano and Potentate, who enjoy a happy retirement at the charity. I mainly looked after two horses, Ravestrey and Penny Max, an Irish Thoroughbred who had won a few races.

I learned how the saddle and bridle worked and how to put them on safely for rider and horse. Over time, I got to understand what the sign in the classroom meant. "Learn from yesterday, live for today, hope for tomorrow".

One day Ira came to see me at Greatwood with her friend who was visiting from America.

"I want to see where you are spending all this time, Abdul!" she said.

I took Ira on a tour of the grounds and introduced her to the cockerels Lunch and Peter Andre. We went and saw the racehorses, who were standing calmly in the field, and I showed her the old milking parlour where I'd mucked out the stalls that morning. Ira was impressed by how much hard work I had put in to making the stalls so clean and tidy for the horses.

Then I showed her the ponies and how they always made a fuss of me when I went in. Ira and her friend tried to come into the enclosure to pet them, but the ponies got jealous when they approached me, snapping and biting at their clothes. One of them even tried to kick Ira's friend.

"They're in love with you, Abdul," Ira said. "They don't want any other ladies getting close to you."

I turned 19 while I was at Greatwood, and in July 2016, a year after I first arrived at the charity, I passed my next 1st4Sport qualification: Entry Level 3 Award in Recognising, Putting on and Cleaning Saddle and Bridle. I also won a Special Progression Award. I was presented with my final certificates at a big leavers' ceremony, which Ira came to, and I met lots of different people from the horse racing industry and community. Lots of owners and jockeys support Greatwood, and I also met Philip Brannan, a horseracing PR consultant who was helping with fundraising. He asked me about my story and where I had come from.

I told him, "I come from Sudan, and now I live in Swindon."

"How did you get to Swindon from Sudan?" Philip asked.

"I walked a lot and I came under a lorry," I said.

We all dressed up smartly for the day, and a photographer came and took pictures of us receiving our certificates. I was prouder of myself that day than I could ever remember.

Even more amazingly, Sasha said Greatwood had found me a place on the Racing Foundation Course at the Northern Racing College in Doncaster, where I could train to be a jockey or a Rider Groom, and that I could spend some time first with the racehorse trainer Nikki Evans at her yard in Abergavenny. I knew by now that all I wanted to do in life was to work with horses, so I accepted nervously. I'd visited Wales with Ira, and I was so happy to be moving away from the hostel and the park bench and into proper accommodation. It was a chance to be away from people altogether and just live in the countryside with horses for company.

Greatwood came at the best possible time for me. The horses gave me a connection to my family and a way back to the person I was when I was seven years old, before anything bad had happened to me. They never judged, always listened, and showed me it was possible to find a place somewhere, wherever you have come from.

The Journey

Somehow, in the space of a year, I went from being a person who wanted to set fire to myself, to someone with a purpose in life.

Abdul at Goodwood races

Chapter Fifteen
Abergavenny

From almost any point on Penbiddle Farm, you can see the Black Mountains stretching away into the distance. When I arrived at the home of Nikki Evans Racing that July, the grass was bright green and the hedgerows were lined with flowers. I would go running out into the foothills and see Wales stretching out in front of me.

The relatively small yard is run by Nikki, the daughter of two Herefordshire trainers and a former jockey who rode a number of winners during her racing career. Her husband Paul is the Assistant Trainer, known for his great horsemanship up on the gallops where the horses train for racing, and for winning over 100 races in South Wales. Together they train horses for racing and for point-to-point races.

When I went there in the late summer, I had spent a year working with and alongside racehorses and riding some of the smaller horses and ponies. I'd learned to ride the mechanical horse and practised my racing position hunched over the reins and using my legs to balance, so the "horse" had the freedom to gallop. But it was while I was with Nikki and Paul that I first learned to ride a racehorse.

At any yard, the horses need riding out each day for exercise and so the trainers can see how they are running. This is called "work". In many stables they'll do fast gallop work twice a week, steady trotting and cantering the rest of the week, and have a rest or a quiet day on a Sunday depending on how near a race is.

The rest of the time they live in a kind of five-star hotel for horses. Many places even have swimming pools and thermal spa areas for the horses, and they are swaddled in blankets and given only the best food that science has devised to eat. Horses have mechanical "walkers" too – treadmills for the horse.

Riding a fit and healthy racehorse is tough work, but you also need to relax, or the horse can sense it. You need good fitness and strong muscles. The first time I rode a racehorse for a mile, even though I could run marathons, I thought I was going to faint when I dismounted. I couldn't walk for days afterwards because the muscles in my legs were so sore.

Riding a racehorse, the stirrups are much shorter than other riders are used to, so that your leg is at a tight right angle, absorbing the shock into your legs instead of the horse's back. The saddle is tiny, so as to weigh as little as possible. From your high-up vantage point, the horse's neck and shoulders appear impossibly muscular. You are aware once again of the extraordinary power of a racehorse even more than when the trainer told you how many times they broke their backs and every bone in their body.

It is tough work being a Rider Groom. In most stables we are up at 6am, work hard until 12, have a two-hour lunchtime break for eating, sleeping and resting and then work until 5.30pm, finally putting the horses to bed at 8pm.

But riding a racehorse is like nothing else on earth. It is like you ride the line between life and death whenever you ride. And there is nothing to beat the feeling of flying along at 40 mph watching the ground blur alongside you, the dirt thickening on your goggles, and feeling as if you and the horse are the same creature.

Riding at Nikki Evans' yard, of course, I was only just getting on a racehorse and learning to walk and canter. But you still feel the incredible power and strength of the animal you are sitting on. One of the other things I learned when I was there was how to lead up a racehorse. This means accompanying a horse to a race, making sure it's ready to perform on the day, and then leading him into and around the parade ring.

Almost a year to the day that I'd started at Greatwood, on 12 August 2016, I led up Monsieur Chevalier, a bay horse, at the 2.50 at Newbury. Monsieur Chevalier travelled in a horse box for nearly three hours from Wales, arriving around three hours before the race so he had time to relax and have a small feed.

It was my job to make sure he and I were looking smart for the occasion. I was in a suit and tie and, when we arrived, I had brushed Monsieur Chevalier's coat until it was gleaming, marking lines into his coat with the brush. An hour before the race, I led him quietly to the pre-parade ring, then to the saddling box where he was saddled up, ready to go. Then came his big moment in the parade ring, where I knew it was important for him to stay calm with all the crowds and noise. As all the people connected to the nine runners in the race gathered in the centre of the parade ring, I walked him round, talking softly to him all the time.

When the bell finally rang for the jockeys to "mount" their racehorses, Nikki came over and gave David Probert, one of the country's top jockeys, a leg up onto the horse. Getting the jockey safely and smoothly on board may look simple, but it's not always straightforward. The horse needs to be kept moving and stay settled while the jockey gets into the saddle and gets his feet into the stirrups. I gave Monsieur Chevalier a reassuring pat on his neck as David jumped onto his back. We made our way onto the horsewalk where the horses are led down in single file, and once we got to the chute I let him go and watched as David cantered him down to the start. Then I walked round to the front of the race with Philip, who was working that day at Newbury, to watch the race.

That day wasn't to be Monsieur Chevalier's. He was going well for most of the race, but finished sixth. The race was only a mile, and was over in what felt like a blinding flash. Afterwards I don't know who was more shocked and exhausted from the adrenalin – me or the horse. Although Monsieur Chevalier, a 66/1 outsider, didn't win the race, I won the cash award for "Best Turned Out Horse", judged by the race sponsors, and I couldn't have been more proud.

Chapter Sixteen
Doncaster

After Penbiddle Farm, I started at the Northern Racing College in Doncaster, now known as the National Racing College. It was one of the most exciting days of my life. An NRC qualification meant I'd have a chance of earning a living as a Rider Groom, which would also give me a roof over my head. Most yards have their own accommodation for staff. I'd be working with the horses every day, riding and taking care of them. It felt like a dream job, and meant I could start to put my fear of being sent back to the hostel behind me.

The first thing I needed to start the course was some kit, which was sponsored by Al Basti Equiworld, a big supporter of Greatwood whose representative Michael O'Hagan I had met when I received my certificates. He had very kindly told Greatwood to get me whatever I wanted. I loved wearing nice clothes, but very rarely had the opportunity to buy any clothes, and never anything new. Now Sasha was driving me to the local country store to choose a proper riding outfit.

I chose black jodhpurs, black leather riding boots and the racing college's navy fleece and polo shirt.

"You're like a kid in a sweet shop," Sasha teased me, seeing how much I liked trying on all the clothes.

A couple of weeks later I was on my way to the stables at the historic Rossington Hall in Doncaster. I hadn't been to the north of England before. It was October, and Doncaster was a few degrees colder than Wiltshire. The college is set in ancient woodland that had already turned orange, red and yellow for the autumn.

The stables where we studied were all in a semi-circular building in the middle, and there was an indoor school where we practised, and tracks in the woodland beyond for us to hack, as well as proper gallops with white railings to develop our riding skills. There were also lots of mechanical horses for us to practise on and get fit enough to ride racehorses.

Even better, there was somewhere clean, safe and dry for us to sleep during our 12-week placement. Meanwhile, the equestrian learning about how to race ride came with lots of practical skills like cookery lessons, support with managing finances, and even how to use a washing machine.

The horse I was paired with was called Rory, a retired grey racehorse better known as Mythical Son during his racing career. He was now 16 years old. Over the three months I was there, I got to know his every mood and whim. I felt the same thing I always felt with old, wise horses, a connection to my past and to my parents just through the experience of grooming Rory.

I enjoyed every part of the 12-week course, whether it was mucking out or riding, and even didn't mind some of the classroom work. I was happy cleaning my boots and putting the horses' blankets on to wash. I didn't mind getting up at 6am, as I was always awake anyway. In general, I found I was sleeping much better with the hard physical exercise, cold fresh air and regular routine. I was eating well because the exercise made me hungry and because they fed us good, healthy food.

I knew I was different from the other students and sometimes I didn't understand their humour or their rapidly spoken English in its different accents. But I was glad to be there, whether riding the horses between the rails so we learned how to keep them running straight during a race, or out hacking in the woods, watching the winter light streaming through the thinning leaves.

When the frost came later that winter, followed by long weeks of deep snow, I was stunned by how beautiful the grounds at Rossington Hall were. I had never seen snow until I was 14 in France, and it still amazed me every time it fell. The 250-acre estate was shared with a stately home that had been a family home, was occupied by the Royal Veterinary Corps and an Indian regiment during World War II, and was used as a missionary training centre for envoys travelling out to Africa. I thought that some of those people must have made the opposite journey from me.

While I was at the Northern Racing College, Philip Brannan, who I'd met at my graduation from Greatwood, came to visit me to tell me he'd entered me for a very special award at the Daily Mirror Pride of Sport Awards.

"Abdul," he told me, "I've been thinking a lot about your story since I met you. I think it's really extraordinary and that's why I've nominated you. To have gone through everything you have in your life, to be an orphan from Darfur and to get to the Northern Racing College and be studying to be a jockey, is incredible."

A few weeks later, I received an invitation to London. The letter said I had been shortlisted for the prestigious Young Achiever Award and was invited to a big ceremony at the Grosvenor House Hotel in Mayfair.

On 19 December 2016, I travelled to London with Matthew Clark, one of my tutors at the Northern Racing

College, and checked into a hotel that was the nicest place I had ever stayed. I put on a smart white shirt and black suit, carefully knotted my tie and went down to the hotel restaurant to meet Philip. Ira was ill at the time, and devastated not to be able to come to the ceremony, but I was very happy to see that Sasha and Helen from Greatwood had come to London for the event.

We were all collected in a smart people carrier and chauffeured the short distance to the Grosvenor House Hotel in Park Lane. The courtyard was brightly lit and full of people and television cameras. Photographers' bulbs flashed as we made our way along a long red carpet towards the reception area. After a short while, we were ushered into the grand ballroom strung with gold chandeliers where the awards ceremony would take place. Waiters with white gloves were serving wine and adjusting table settings.

"I can't believe that a year ago I was living in a hostel," I whispered to Philip.

Inside the ballroom were table after table of sports stars and famous people. I didn't know who many of them were, but I did recognise racing presenter Ollie Bell, who sat next to me on our table.

Philip explained that the awards were to honour the "unsung heroes" of grassroots sport and the elite heroes who inspire them.

"Maybe you'll win, Abdul," he said.

Because of being nominated for the award, a journalist had come to interview me at the Northern Racing College for the *Daily Mirror*, and a photographer had come to take portraits of me riding Rory in the indoor school and in the beautiful autumn grounds outside. Philip showed me the big double-page spread in the newspaper, with a large photograph of me sitting on Rory, wearing the purple and green colours of the Northern Racing College. The headline said: "Inspirational jockey reveals how riding helps him feel close to his parents slaughtered in brutal conflict". Everyone had a copy of the newspaper and I could see them reading it and looking at me.

We ate a very nice dinner, and then it was time for the awards. It was interesting to hear about everyone else's achievements. There was Dame Kelly Holmes, the Olympic gold medallist, who had set up a trust to help disadvantaged children, England rugby coach Eddie Jones, and the Paralympian Sarah Storey. The Team Award went to Team GB and Paralympian Team GB for their record-breaking medal haul at the 2016 Rio Olympics.

Then came my award. I only realised I had won when everyone started clapping and standing up at my table. I was very nervous when I had to go and collect it from the stage.

The host Ben Shephard told everyone, "Abdul has faced an unimaginable battle just to be here today at all."

They showed a video about my life that had some images in it from the conflict in Darfur. I hadn't looked at any photographs of Darfur in a long time, and I didn't know what to feel. It added to the surreal sense of standing there in a big, expensive room under bright lights so many thousands of miles from my home.

The video was narrated by Clare Balding, the sports presenter from a big racing family.

"What Abdul has gone through is simply unimaginable," Clare Balding said. "But his story shows the incredible power of sport to bring people together and help them to heal, even after the most appalling suffering."

The Young Achiever Award was presented by Lee Pearson, the Paralympic dressage gold medallist. It meant a lot because Lee is disabled and has been on his own difficult journey to be able to ride horses. "We know how small the planet is when we do sport," Lee said. He told the audience I was "truly inspirational". I didn't know where to look, but I was glad that Philip came on stage with me.

Then, on the stage, Ben Shephard asked me who my biggest hero was in horseracing. It is hands down Frankie Dettori, the Italian racing jockey who famously rode all seven winners on British Champions Day at Ascot in 1996.

The son of a jockey, he left school at 13 to become an apprentice jockey and stable lad. I love his energy and his cheeky smile, and the way he has broken so many records.

Ben said Frankie Dettori couldn't be there, but he had a message for me. They played a video of Frankie speaking to me. I couldn't believe it.

"I came to Britain as a young man with a dream, and through our shared love of horses this country took me to its heart and I am proud to call it home," Frankie said. "It is impossible to imagine what Abdul has been through to get here but now Britain, and the horseracing world in particular, has given him a home and a purpose in life.

"We read so much about what divides us, but sports and especially Abdul's incredible story show us what we have in common. Whether you are born in Sudan, Milan or in Milton Keynes, sport really can break down barriers and bring us together.

"And Abdul, congratulations – you have shown so much strength in getting this far, nothing can stop you from reaching your dream. But Abdul, please: don't break my records!"

Everyone laughed when Frankie said that. On stage, Ben Shephard asked me about what I loved about horses. I was struggling with my English in front of the cameras and under the bright lights.

I told him: "Sometimes I feel myself I am a horse."

Afterwards I chatted to some of the other winners and presenters, who wanted to hear everything about my journey from Sudan and how I had come to be studying at the Northern Racing College. Then Olympic champion Dame Kelly Holmes came and asked if she could have a selfie with me, which I found very funny.

Abdul with his Young Achiever Award at
the Pride of Sport Awards

Chapter Seventeen
Kingsclere

My time at the Northern Racing College seemed to go very quickly, and I graduated in January 2017. The next step was to try to get another work placement with a racing stables, and Philip had an idea. Clare Balding had done the voice-over for my video at the Pride of Sport Awards, and her family had a very well-known yard at Kingsclere near Basingstoke, which would bring me back near Swindon again. Clare and her brother Andrew are the children of one of the greatest ever trainers in the country, Ian Balding, and now Andrew runs the stables and is a successful trainer in his own right.

Philip said he would ask Andrew and his wife Anna Lisa if they might take me on as a Rider Groom at Park House Stables in Kingsclere. At that time, the apprentice rider Kayleigh Stephens, who was employed by Park House, was finishing a short course at the Northern Racing College, and she kindly agreed to drive me back down to Hampshire with her.

The interview day in early February was a cold, clear day. Like Greatwood, Kingsclere is on the North Wessex Downs, in a stunning area of natural beauty. Just over the ridgeway, which the trainers use for the gallops, is the famous Watership Down at Ecchinswell, where the story about the rabbits searching for safety was set by Richard Adams. On one side it rises steeply, giving magnificent views across the Downs, and on the other it slopes gently down towards Park House stables.

Kingsclere itself is about as English a village as you could imagine, with a Georgian high street, pubs and a church that dates back to Norman times. Its weather-vane has a bed bug on it, from when King John is said to have had a restless night in the Kingsclere Inn. After all the years I spent in bedbug-ridden hostels and doss houses, my body covered with bites, I like to think I have something in common with King John.

We arrived early, and two heavy wooden gates swung open to let Kayleigh's car onto the gravel drive. As we turned the corner, a magnificent house came into view with huge sash windows and walls covered in green leaves. Ivy climbed up two columns either side of the front door, with lawns in front and a garden just visible beyond.

Kayleigh and I went around to a side door, where an office of accountants and administrators were busy on telephones and behind computer screens. We waited, and were eventually ushered into a bright, light kitchen to meet Anna Lisa Balding, Andrew's wife, the powerhouse who runs so much of Park House stables. I could see lots of pictures of the couple's children around the place, and a giant boxer dog pushed past me on its way to a different room.

"So you want to be a jockey, Abdul?" Anna Lisa said.

I nodded nervously. My eye was on the giant boxer dog, which was the size of a small pony. At that time, I still hated dogs, and they filled me with fear as a bad omen. I hoped the dog being there didn't mean I wouldn't get the job.

"That's Tonto," Anna Lisa said. "Don't mind him."

After that, Andrew's assistant Nigel Walker took me on a tour of Park House Stables. I had never been in a yard so vast, or with so many horses. Park House had trained Triple Crown winners here as early as the 1800s and the red-brick stables were built in Victorian times for the sole purpose of keeping Thoroughbred racehorses happy, healthy and relaxed, and away from distractions. Nigel told me that Andrew Balding, like his father Ian before him, even trained horses for Her Majesty the Queen.

Each spacious stable has stone double walls to keep horses warm in winter and cool in summer. Staff were walking busily around, leading horses, carrying saddles or washing, or mucking out, dressed in riding boots and smart navy blue sweatshirts and baseball hats emblazoned with a "K" for Kingsclere. I could hear the metallic tap of Eugene the farrier working on horses' hooves ringing out across the cobbled stone of the yards.

Nigel said there were 199 stables at Kingsclere.

"That's a lot of hooves," I thought.

We stopped to see various horses, all strong, beautiful, curious animals who snuffled into my neck and nibbled my hands. One handsome brown horse with a white flash across his nose took a shine to me, nipping my neck.

"That's Beat The Bank, owned by Leicester City football club's owners," Nigel said. "He's new. I think he's going to be one of our biggest superstars." As I stroked his nose, I wondered how many million pounds of horse I was stroking and how many races he would win.

Beat The Bank and I arrived at Park House Stables at the same time, and I always loved that horse. He did go on to be one of Park House's biggest superstars, but sadly he is no longer with us. Beat The Bank was fatally injured after bravely winning at Ascot in July 2019. A year before his death, his owners, including club chairman Vichai Srivaddhanaprabha, had died in a tragic helicopter crash at Leicester City's ground. We were all heartbroken at Kingsclere.

At Park House, as at any racing yard, the horses are the pampered rock stars and the humans' buildings are functional. There's a hostel for the young Rider Grooms with bedrooms upstairs. The communal area has a neat kitchen and battered sofas, and mechanical horses set in front of a television so you can ride along during a race. All of this is overseen by the House Mother, who looks after the young people. When we came through the kitchen, she was preparing a delicious-smelling lunch for the riders when they came in from their morning rides. I felt hungry just walking through there.

Then we went into the tack room, where a stream of young people were consulting the lists for the day, telling them which horses they were to ride and which "lot" to ride them in. I thought of my name, "Abdul", being up on that chart next to the names of famous horses. For now, everyone looked incredibly busy and didn't give me a second glance.

In the biggest yard stood the statue to Mill Reef, the horse that saw Andrew and Clare's father Ian named champion trainer in 1971. The famous racehorse won the Derby, Eclipse, King George and was even flown in a military plane to win the Prix de l'Arc de Triomphe in France that year.

Nigel explained that Mill Reef's life had been saved on one occasion in the Colours Room, where the owners' registered colours are kept. He showed me the room itself, which was full of the bright silks of some of the famous families and dynasties whose horses live at Kingsclere, including Her Majesty the Queen. I imagined the huge body of Mill Reef lying on the floor being treated by a desperate veterinary surgeon, and him coming back to life. The horse's owner, Paul Mellon, was so grateful to Ian Balding that when he died, he left his trademark black and gold colours to the Kingsclere Racing Club.

After the Colours Room, we drove out in a Land Rover to the low gallops, where riders run the horses out each day. Horses are divided into four lots, meaning riders might ride out up to four times on different horses. This was "fourth lot" – the last ride just before horses and riders break for lunchtime. The horses were powering along the low gallops by a white fence, and it was clear there were some brilliant young riders thundering along.

"So, Abdul, what do you think of Park House?" Anna Lisa asked, as we walked back out of the stables' gates and back towards the house her family lived in. It was a beautiful winter's afternoon with bare trees framing a cold blue sky.

I felt overwhelmed by shyness, but eventually managed to speak.

"It's wonderful," I said.

"Well, why don't you come and work here and see how you get on?" Anna Lisa said.

I started at Kingsclere two weeks later, and life became a blur of hard physical work and responsibility. I initially had two horses I was responsible for exercising each day and keeping clean, fed and watered, under the watchful eye of Nigel. I was up at 5.30am every day, which was no problem for me as I still hardly ever slept, and the slightest noise would startle me awake. Adrenalin would pump fast around my body until I slowly realised I wasn't on a park bench or sleeping under a bush or in a warzone with bombs landing around me, but in a safe single bed in my little room in the Kingsclere hostel. There was no way I could get back to sleep after that, though, so I would just put the light on and make clay animals or watch news reports about Africa until 5.30am.

Riding a racehorse is one of the most physically demanding jobs imaginable, and riding out twice at such speed was shattering. Even my long periods of running marathons and good general fitness, and all the riding at the Northern Racing College, hadn't prepared me for the agonising build-up of lactic acid that happens in your legs when you ride a racehorse properly. I found that I was hungry for good food in a way that I had never felt, and that my mind was often blissfully empty of thoughts because I was so tired. As I got to know the two horses I was looking after, Seeusoon and Sea Sculpture, I also made two important friendships. Whatever was happening with my mental health, which was always up and down, and the nightmares and flashbacks I still regularly experienced, those two horses always sensed it, and lifted me up, calming me as I calmed them. The closeness I felt to them as I brushed, fed, rode and cared for them was like the closeness I remembered with our family's animals when I was a child. We weren't different species; we were all a family.

After a while I was given extra horses to look after and ride too. At certain times of the year, different riders are away, and their horses are divided amongst us to look after.

But my favourite was Seeusoon, a bay colt not even a year old when I started at Kingsclere. The foal of Sea The Moon and Village Fete, he was spirited and could still be naughty, trying to nip the horses running alongside him.

"Don't be rude, Seeusoon," I would whisper to him. "Be a good boy."

At that time, I was riding five lots some days – Sea Sculpture, Dudley Boy, Essendon, Seeusoon and a filly called Silver Swift. I even went with the horses to be gelded, to calm them when they had the quick operation. It reminded me of the time I was given my scars in Darfur to show that I was a Zaghawa tribesman and which group of nomads I came from. Except we didn't have anaesthetic in Darfur.

One day, I was riding Seeusoon around the concrete doughnut of the Indoor School, a big ring of breezeblocks the horses rode through where six laps equalled a mile, when I saw Anna Lisa waiting to speak to me. I pulled up after finishing my laps and dismounted.

The Head Trainer nodded to me that I could go. Seeusoon had been running well that day.

"Abdul," she said, "there's a very special visitor today. I'd like you to come and meet her. Make sure your uniform looks smart and put some clean boots on."

I led Seeusoon back to his stall and quickly went to wash my hands and change from my work boots to a clean pair.

"Hurry up, Abdul," one of the grooms shouted. "Anna Lisa says to come now."

I walked the short distance to the stud yard at the front of the stables, where I could see a number of people had gathered. A Range Rover with blacked out windows was parked nearby. Inside the yard, there was an older lady in a raincoat with a headscarf tied around her head. I wondered if that could be the special person? She looked very ordinary, in a skirt and cardigan, like somebody's nice grandmother.

"Who is that?" I whispered to one of the grooms while the lady greeted a tall black racehorse with obvious pleasure, her eyes darting along the horse's gleaming coat and wide, curious eyes.

"Her Majesty the Queen!" the groom whispered back.

The Queen seemed to have come just with a driver and one other man.

"That's John Warren," the groom said. "The Queen's Racing Manager."

One by one, each of her horses was led in so she could see them moving. Andrew Balding was speaking to her earnestly, and from the discussion it was very clear she was extremely knowledgeable about each animal she was being introduced to, almost like another trainer.

Anna Lisa called me over to her.

"Abdul, could you lead King's Lynn around the paddock, please?"

I was very nervous, but I concentrated on making King's Lynn look his best, leading him as calmly as I could around the paddock. I didn't look at the Queen right until the end. I could have sworn that she smiled at me.

I was always aware of race days at Kingsclere because horses would go off with great excitement, racing gear, horses and lads for the day's race all loaded up into a horsebox lorry. But the horses I looked after were young colts and didn't begin racing until they were around two years old, after intensive riding and training. My horses, as I now thought of them, started being entered for races towards the end of that year, 2017, and were racing in earnest by 2018.

The first horse to race out of those I cared for and rode daily was Silver Swift, a bay filly who was entered into the 6.10 at Kempton Racecourse on 4 October 2017. The jockey was David Probert, who had ridden Monsieur Chevalier, the horse I had led up at my very first race for Nikki Evans back when I lived in Abergavenny. That morning, we loaded up Silver Swift into the horsebox, ready for the hour or so's journey from Kingsclere. She was clearly nervous, and I spoke to her gently, reassuring her that this was going to be one of the best, most exciting days of her life.

When we got there, Leanne the Travelling Head Girl helped me check the racehorse over for loose shoes or any bumps during the journey. Then she called me over.

"Come on, Abdul," she said. "We're going to run the track."

I love to run and was happy to set off with her along the track. Leanne said we were checking the condition of the ground – was it heavy, hard, soft, good to soft, good to firm or firm? – and checking the rails to make sure they were all in the right place. Andrew had arrived by now, and he and Leanne saddled up Silver Swift while David weighed out. I whispered good luck to the filly, and stroked her beautiful deep brown coat and the white flash down her nose. I think she was calming me down as much as I was calming her.

David wore light blue, dark blue and white colours that looked smart on the racecourse as they lined up with the other racehorses, ready to go. I could see that Silver Swift was nervous. Nothing can prepare a racehorse for this moment.

The race seemed to only take seconds, and it was all my brain could do to hold onto David's blue and black hat.

Silver Swift wasn't last in the race, but she was always to the rear and came in 10th. It would be a year before she finally won her first race, at Salisbury Races, when Jason Watson rode her to victory.

After the race, I walked Silver Swift until she had cooled down, washed her gleaming back of sweat, and then there was an hour's rest for the horse while Leanne collected the colours from the weighing room and we all drank a cup of tea. I checked the horse over for any injuries, but she didn't have any.

"Don't tell me you just didn't feel like winning today," I whispered to her.

When we got back to the yard it was already late, and we still had to hose out the lorry and put all the racing gear away, and lead Silver Swift back to her lodgings.

Andrew is a talented trainer with a world-class stables, and since then my horses have won many times at the races, and I have come to know quite well whether they are likely to win or not depending on the mood they are in. The bond between Rider Groom and horse is known to be one of the most important relationships in a racehorse's life, and when we win, the jockey and owner will often give us a tip from his winnings.

One of my proudest wins came in July 2019, when the Irish jockey Oisin Murphy won on the bay filly Shadn. I was very smart that day in a shirt and tie, and Oisin was in a pink, white, blue and yellow jersey. It was the only race of the day where there was also a prize for the groom, and I felt incredibly proud going up to accept the award with Oisin and Andrew.

Abdul at the Daily Mirror Pride of Sport Awards, 19 December 2016

Chapter Eighteen
Norway

While all of these things were happening in my life, I never stopped looking for Yusuf, scouring the internet and posting in different search groups, and joining every refugee reunion scheme I could find. In 2015 I had gone to Calais. In 2017, I saved up and went to France again with friends, this time to look through different ports on the south coast for him, using my ID card to travel inside the EU. On that trip I continued to see Yusuf at a distance everywhere – standing on docks, in the parks, standing around fires at night in the countryside. But it was never him. It was another 18-year-old boy from Africa. A different Yusuf.

In 2019, I went with my friends to Norway. They were people I had met through the mosque in Swindon, who were also missing relatives. They said Norway had taken lots of Darfuri refugees and people from Libya around the time I was trying to escape the continent of Africa.

I flew for the first time in a jumbo jet, high in the sky, alongside the clouds – a completely different experience from when I used to fly in the light aircraft above Liddington. Down below me, I had the strangest sense of the planet I had crossed, as if for all those eight years I had just been a tiny ant being pushed back by the wind and the waves.

When my ears started popping painfully, I completely panicked and called over the air stewardess.

"Something is happening to my ears!" I shouted.

I was screaming with pain. I thought my brain was bursting out of my ears and I was really frightened.

"It's very normal when the plane is going up or coming down," the air stewardess said, giving me a boiled sweet. I was glad that in all my travels I had never tried to stow away on a plane.

In Norway, we visited different places where there were said to be large communities of Sudanese migrants, but we didn't find Yusuf and nobody had heard of him. We travelled on buses and marvelled at the landscape of fir trees, fjords and fishing villages – a cold, wet, steep land even more alien to Africans than France or the UK.

One day I was out running through the Norwegian countryside when I saw the familiar sight of a string of racehorses galloping along with riders hanging on tightly. I followed the route the horses took and came to what appeared to be a busy yard on the edge of a clearing.

I walked up the long drive and knocked at the front door. The man who answered looked a bit surprised to see me, a black man with no vehicle standing in his shorts on the doorstep.

"My name is Abdul," I said. "I'm from England. I was wondering if I could ride one of your horses, please? I'm in Norway on holiday."

The man smiled kindly. "Well, these are very expensive horses to be taking out riding," he said, with a strong Nordic accent. "But I can direct you to a riding school somewhere nearby."

"I don't want to ride ponies," I said. "I want to ride racehorses. I'm a jockey, and I am getting out of shape on my holidays."

The man looked at me more seriously. "You're a jockey?" he repeated. "Which trainer?"

"Park House Stables," I said. "With Andrew Balding. He's one of the best trainers in the world."

"I know who Andrew Balding is," the man said. "You'd better come in, Abdul."

I told the man a bit of my story and how I'd come to the UK and got off a lorry in Swindon and luckily that was where a lot of UK horseracing went on. He went and found me some spare kit to wear and introduced me to the Head Lad.

"Let's give you Lightning to ride first," he said. "She's fast, but she's getting on a bit. See how you get on."

I stroked Lightning's nose and whispered a bit in her ear. I could tell she liked me, as she hardly moved when I put the saddle on her.

I rode Lightning out that day, an exhilarating ride through the Norwegian forest and along the top of a fjord, some of the most stunning landscape I had ever seen. After not riding for a couple of weeks, my breath was ragged and my legs were burning when I got back to the stables.

For the last week of my holiday I rode the stable's horses every day, sometimes two or three of them, and at the end, the man – who turned out to be one of the most famous trainers in Norway – offered me a job.

"Any time you want to move to Norway, you'll have work here, Abdul," he said, wishing me good luck in my search for Yusuf.

I thanked him.

"I like working for my boss Andrew Balding," I said. "But if I ever need to come back to Norway again looking for my brother I will come and ride for you."

Back at Park House, I spent the rest of the summer revising for my Citizenship Test between races and work. It was very confusing. I learned that England, Scotland and Wales form Great Britain, but that you need Northern Ireland to make the United Kingdom. I learned that Prime Minister's Questions is held once a week, William Shakespeare was born in a place called Stratford-upon-Avon, and that King Charles I was executed. I learned about voter registration systems, haggis and the Black Death.

When I asked my fellow riders for help with the questions, they just laughed. "How would I know who established the Church of England?" one lad said to me.

I learned all the Kings and Queens of England and Scotland, and the date of the Queen's Silver Jubilee, while living at close quarters with Her Majesty's horse King's Lynn at Kingsclere.

On June 19, my amazing Shadn, one of the most promising horses I looked after, had her first race at Royal Ascot. As I led Shadn up, I could see the figure of Her Majesty in the distance.

Shadn didn't win that day, but on 12 September, King's Lynn carried the HRH's royal purple and regal red colours to victory at the 3.15 at Doncaster, in a prestigious £300,000 race. Oisin Murphy was once again in the saddle. At 12-1, King's Lynn was the least experienced runner in the field, but burst clear at the final furlong, with a length in hand at the finish.

"He's absolutely flying," Oisin said – and so was everyone at Park House. We watched the race on the television back at the yard, clapping and cheering.

The next month, Shadn went on to win in France at the Criterium de Maisons-Laffitte after running a fantastic race. Andrew said Shadn was going to go to America for the summer and, if I could get a passport, maybe I could go and visit her.

That evening I lay on my bed thinking about whether Shadn would have to go on an aeroplane to America and whether she would be frightened or excited. I wondered whether she would like being there, where her American sire No Nay Never is from. Perhaps, for her, it would feel like going home. I thought about how Shadn, a racehorse, could travel to any country she had a race in, while I was both safe but also trapped by my refugee status.

Shadn didn't have to learn the Kings and Queens of England to travel abroad or run at Royal Ascot. To get a passport and visit her, I would need to pass my Citizenship Test.

I thought of all the many places I had been and the countries and cultures I had passed through. I wondered if I might one day travel the world again, as a free British citizen. In the morning, I stood with Shadn for a long time, thinking about how much I would miss her when she went.

Epilogue

My alarm goes off at 5.45am on Tuesday 22 October 2019, even earlier than usual. I'm off to Norfolk today with Seeusoon. He's being quite naughty as usual, refusing to load in, and nipping at me as he goes up into the horsebox. He's running in the 3.25 at Yarmouth, a racecourse I've never been to before. It's quite far from Kingsclere – over four hours in a normal car and six at the speed we need to travel to keep the horses calm.

The next day is a really big day for me, and I'm hoping we're not going to be back too late from Great Yarmouth. Ira and Philip have both told me to have a nice early night. I had no idea the racecourse was going to be so far, but I'd never miss a race day. Seeusoon needs me, and so does Andrew.

"Don't worry, boy," I tell Seeusoon as I load in hay and water and we lock up the trailer. He's not a good traveller, but he'll be okay with some breaks in the journey.

Everyone is in a good mood on the journey. On Sunday there was a huge party for the staff at Kingsclere.

Park House had a massive win at the weekend at Ascot with Donjuan Triumphant, a first group one win for King Power. Andrew had tears in his eyes at the finish, because it was a week to the year since Donjuan's former owner Vichai Srivaddhanaprabha died in the helicopter crash at Leicester City.

"He would have loved this," I saw Andrew say on television.

The long journey makes me think of all the long trips I've been on in my life. It's only six hours and travelling in the trailer isn't uncomfortable, but watching the roads and people and countryside slip by, I think of all the places I've travelled. I'm 22 now, but I spent eight years travelling between Darfur and the UK, and it's been seven years now since I arrived. The last couple of years I have been travelling safely with my horses, zigzagging across the British Isles. Those journeys have been some of the best of my life.

We get to Yarmouth eventually around lunchtime, with a couple of hours to spare until the race. The racecourse is only 500 yards from the beach, which I wasn't expecting.

"You're right at the edge of the country here," one of the race staff says to me. "There's only sea and eventually the rest of the world out there. If you kept going you'd get to Denmark."

It's a glorious sunny day, cold but bright, not a cloud in the sky. I grab my lunch from the horsebox and walk down towards the sea. I skirt the golf course and pass through a caravan site. It's half term, and there are children everywhere, enjoying the chance to be outdoors after a rainy few days, kicking footballs, and running around.

After a few minutes I come out onto the North Dene sand dunes and the windswept shoreline beyond. The sky is enormous, with nothing to challenge it in any direction. Behind me, the soft dunes are held back by thick patches of wiry grass. In front of me, a flat beach slopes only very slightly towards the waves spotted with stones and knots of seaweed. Beyond that there is only lapping white waves where the water of the world meets the sandy shore. In the far distance I can see a line of white wind turbines. I'm alone except for a hungry-looking black-and-white dog chasing the waves and barking at seagulls he will never catch, and which look almost as big as him.

Yusuf is out there somewhere across that sea. I shout his name.

"Yusuf!"

But there is only the wind to hear me.

By 2pm, I'm leading Seeusoon round the pre-parade ring so he can warm up his muscles, get the blood flowing, and ease any stiffness from his long journey. He's saddled up by Andrew, and then I lead him to the Parade Ring so the punters can get a good look at him before the race. The other horses look in fine fettle, glowing coats and bright eyes, but Seeusoon is in form too, if he chooses to be.

Martin Dwyer, the jockey, arrives and chats to Andrew and Seeusoon's owner about last-minute tactics. Then they call the 3.25 racers to the starting stalls. It's time for the race.

Seeusoon is never even in the running today. He finishes 11th out of 11, and that's only because two horses didn't run at all. When Martin dismounts, I think of all the races I've been to over the last two years. I stroke Seeusoon's nose, and rub his face.

"What was that about, Seeusoon?" I ask him. "You did so bad today!"

He looks at me as if to say, "You put me in a horsebox for six hours."

I shake my head and take him for a shower. "The next race you are going to try harder and win."

I'm letting Seeusoon relax for a bit when I see a commotion going on over at the racecourse, and run over to see what's happening. The horse Jean Valjean, running in the 4.30, has broken loose from the track. His jockey Sean Kirrane manages to jump off the horse just before it smashes through the white fence, escaping onto the golf course beyond.

One of the racecourse staff is laughing until he's crying.

"He's called Jean Valjean," he tells me. "Jean Valjean!"

I don't see the joke.

"You don't know who that is," he says. "He's the French revolutionary from *Les Miserables*. Of course he's gone and made a bolt for freedom!"

I still don't know what he means, but I smile at him anyway. He's got a funny laugh. As I walk back to Seeusoon, I wonder if Jean Valjean's done what I did and made a break for the beach and the cold sea on a sunny day. Maybe, like me, he's looking for someone important to him.

With all the commotion, it's 6pm before we get Seeusoon back into the horsebox and our convoy back on the road. It's going to be six hours before we get back to Park House. So much for an early night. The sun is just setting as we reach the long flat road to Norwich, and in the last streak of red before darkness, the horizon seems wider and higher than ever, with birds circling and swooping down onto the Broads.

On the radio we hear that Jean Valjean made it through the golf course, through several people's gardens and all the way to the beach, before heading four miles along the sea to between Scratby and Caister. I thought how free he must have felt running along the beach with sand under his hooves, but his trainer said he'd been injured in his break for freedom, his legs covered with scratches and bruises. He was now, the news announcer said, being slowly walked back to the track.

For the rest of the journey we keep the radio on, listening to all the old songs, ones I know from the radio in the yard. Soon we are just moving in blackness through the flat countryside where hardly a single light shines. I am aware of the water and fields passing, and all the animals getting ready for the night and the people coming in from work.

As the horsebox lumbers along, I think as I always do of travelling in the people traffickers' truck from Libya across the sands of the Sahara. I think of the long walk to Chad over many days and nights from my parents' burned village in Darfur. The journey from the border up to Ajdabiya and eventually north to Tripoli. The boat crossing over the wild sea from Libya to France. Finally, the lorry from France to England. What had I thought of during that treacherous journey, clinging on above the lorry's wheel? I can no longer remember. I can only think of now, trundling through the blackness in a warm cabin with the radio on and a flask of hot tea and voices chatting next to me. I'm safe enough to fall asleep, my head bumping along to the rise and fall of the road.

The alarm goes off again at 5.45am the next day. I only got to bed at 1am after seeing Seeusoon safely to his stable, but I forgot to change the alarm from the previous morning. Luckily, I need to be up early today in any case.

I go down in my T-shirt and shorts to use the iron in the grooms' room to get my shirt smartly ironed, and then bring my black suit out of the wardrobe, the one I use on special occasions at the racecourse. Then I go down and eat breakfast. After breakfast I get all my smart clothes on, admire myself in the mirror and decide I need a haircut. I can get one in Swindon, on the way in. For a moment I stand looking at the clay animals on my windowsill – the elephants, giraffe and lions I have made over the years whenever I can get my hands on clay or mud. They remind me of a childhood spent modelling clay animals in the riverbed. Even though I made them here, they are one of the very few objects I own that link to my past.

When I go back downstairs, I get a few comments and wolf whistles from the other riders.

"Look at you, Abdul!" they shout.

It's 9am when I finally set off from the stables to the bus stop. Andrew and Anna Lisa's driver stops me as I get to the gate.

"I'll give you a lift to the station, Abdul," he says. "It's your big day, isn't it?"

I get to Swindon by 11am, long before I am due to meet all the others. As I walk through the pedestrianised town centre I feel immediately anxious, mixed emotions swirling around my head. Swindon has been many places to me. It's where I came off a lorry. It is where I slept on the streets. It's where I was arrested by the police. It's where I found sanctuary.

Ira meets me at midday and we go to the barbers'. They do a very neat job on my hair. I get into her car and we drive to a nice place for lunch.

On the radio is a story that makes me clap my hand over my mouth. I feel sick to my stomach. I'm shaking. 39 people have been found dead in the back of a refrigerated lorry in Essex. 39 people who have frozen or suffocated to death. Migrants like me, who were seeking a better life. Who chose almost certain death by crossing the channel in danger, over a life of servitude and debt where they were.

The man on the radio is talking about the effect on the emergency services who had to open that lorry and bring the people out. I am thinking of their last moments on that lorry. How did they feel? Did they know they were dying? Were they clawing at the sides of the lorry in desperation, banging on the sides? Did they hold hands?

We don't know this yet, but among the 39 Vietnamese people who died that day are 10 teenagers, including two boys the same age I was when I came under a lorry into the UK. Dinh Dinh Binh from Hai Phong province was 15 years old. So was Nguyen Huy Hung, a serious-looking boy from Ha Tinh province, who had made a long journey through Russia and Poland hoping to join his parents in the UK.

I think about their families, waiting desperately for the news their loved ones have arrived safely, wondering if their children are already standing on the brink of a new life. People ringing mobile phones that had frozen or might be answered by a British voice, a voice that could only mean the worst.

Ira snaps off the radio as we reached the pub.

"Oh, Abdul," she says. Her eyes are full of tears.

At the pub, Ira's daughter Rachel and little five-year-old grandson Jamie are waiting. It is wonderful to see them both. Rachel is 34 now. Ira's daughters Rachel and George will never replace Yusuf and my sisters who died, Sharifa and Amina, but they are my family for life now. Jamie lets me lift him up and swing him round and cuddle him. He wants to sit on my shoulders all the time.

We eat lunch and Ira teases me about the healthy food I choose.

"I'm a jockey," I tell her. "I have to be careful what I eat!"

I tell her I've stopped drinking tea because I'm trying to see if I can sleep better. Ira always thinks I'm funny whatever I tell her.

At 2pm, Ira looks at her watch.

"Oh God, Abdul," she says. "We're going to be late!"

We all squeeze into Ira's tiny car and make our way to the council offices. I've been there many times before. It's where I did all my age assessment interviews and it's where I saw social services. I think back to the frightened 15-year-old boy I was then, and the 22-year-old man I am now in a smart suit and a fresh haircut.

On the steps of the offices we meet Chris, my original social worker, who I have kept in touch with all these years, and Philip. We all hug. We are in the building next to the one where I did my interviews with Chris.

Then it's into the corridor, following the big signs. Eventually we get to the room.

"Citizenship Ceremonies", it says over the door. Today is the day I'm going to become British.

After I have handed over my ID card and confirmed I will swear my oath, we are shown into a plush anteroom packed with people. The patterned carpet and wallpaper make my eyes go a bit dizzy. Eventually all of the people becoming British citizens that day are ushered into a big, wood-panelled council chamber. Our seats, where the councillors would usually sit, are all marked with our names. We are seated in alphabetical order so mine is the first name, at the very front – Abdulkareem Adam.

Just in front of me is a portrait of Queen Elizabeth II, with a raised Union Jack next to it. She seems to be smiling at me. I smile back. There can't be many other people in here who have actually met her in person.

Next, they ask all the family and friends of the people who are being made citizens to come through into the chamber. There are lots of them. Husbands, wives, children, parents. They are all looking so smart, as if they are at a wedding. Little boys in suits, and little girls in dresses. It feels like the whole world is here – black, white, Muslim, Christian, African, Arabic, Asian, European and everything besides.

As they file in, patriotic classical music is playing, as if we are at a concert. Then a man in a frock coat leads in the dignitaries. He is carrying a ceremonial mace, which he lays in front of the Mayor of Swindon.

"Today, we are here to formally welcome 45 new citizens to this nation and to our community in Swindon," says the Superintendent Registrar, who thanks us for adding to Swindon's rich diversity. She says there are people here from 22 countries and lists them, some near and some far. Afghanistan, Vietnam, Poland, Nepal, Zimbabwe, Italy – and, of course, Sudan. "A small part of the world is here, just in this room," she says. "I know some of you have had to wait a very long time to be here. But this is the last step in the process of becoming a British citizen."

The Deputy Lord Lieutenant of Wiltshire, Shirley Ludford, explains she is here to represent the Queen at our ceremony. She tells us all about the wider county – how Salisbury is the home of the Magna Carta, which we learned about for our citizenship test, and the standing stones at Stonehenge.

The Mayor of Swindon, Kevin Parry, tells us we can all vote now in any elections in Britain. "And I hope you will," he says. He talks to us about the coat of arms of Swindon with the swan representing the river. He says the town's motto means "Health and Industry" – "and I would like to wish you an abundance of both".

We all swear the oath together to be "a faithful citizen not just today, but into the future", and true allegiance to Her Majesty the Queen, her heirs and successors. Then we take the pledge of commitment. "I will give my loyalty to the UK and respect its rights and freedoms," I say along with 44 others. "I will uphold its democratic values. I will observe its laws faithfully and fulfil my duties and obligations as a British citizen."

While I'm saying the words, I'm thinking of all the other people in the room. The hopes and dreams they have come to Britain with, and what little else. How many came like me with nothing but the clothes they stood up in? Who came by plane with a ticket and a passport? Who came under lorries or across stormy seas? Who lost friends and family to war and violence along the way? Who was trafficked? Who came for work? Who simply came for love?

I think of those 22 countries – Afghanistan, Vietnam, Poland, Nepal, Zimbabwe and all the rest – and of the things happening there. And then I think of the 39 people entombed in that desperate lorry in Essex. The 39 and all the other lost ones, the thousands upon thousands who didn't make it here.

I think of Yusuf – always Yusuf – and for a moment the pain is overwhelming. Did he make it to a safe country? Is he living in a dusty shack in Chad or a Libyan prison or a cold French street, or did he get into a lorry where there was no air to breathe?

When we are all seated, the Mayor and the Deputy Lord Lieutenant move to the front of the chamber. We are all called up one by one. I am the first person to become British today. Adam, the first man.

I walk to the front, holding my head high, and take the certificate they hand me. This is it. I am British. I am safe. I have rights. No-one can ever deport me. I am not home, but I have a home, and that home is Britain.

I look over at Ira in the audience and she is crying. When they take the official photograph, I am beaming, a wide smile right across my face.

Afterwards we are invited for tea and biscuits in the hall behind the council chamber. Except there isn't any tea. I drink water instead and eat several of those very English biscuits with cream and sticky jam in the middle. Old habits die hard.

Ira introduces me to the Deputy Lord Lieutenant for Wiltshire.

"This is Abdul," she tells her. "You both work for the Queen."

The Deputy Lord Lieutenant looks round at me.

"Do you work for the Queen, Abdul?"

"Yes," I say, hurriedly swallowing my biscuit. "I'm a jockey. Our stables look after five of the Queen's horses."

Like a lot of British people, and especially anyone connected to the Queen, the Deputy Lord Lieutenant for Wiltshire turns out to be keen on horseracing. I say I will look out for her next time I am at Newbury, but I'm not allowed to give any tips, as it's against the rules. I think she looks a bit disappointed.

"I'm from Sudan," I tell her, as a kind of explanation about why I'm here today becoming a British citizen. "From Darfur."

"What do you think of Wiltshire?" the Deputy Lord Lieutenant says.

"It's good," I say.

I wonder again how I had the luck to be found under a lorry in Wiltshire, with its eight chalk white horses, and its love of racing. Maybe Walid the Tunisian smuggler was right, and God was looking after me. I hope, until I find my brother, He is looking after Yusuf too.

Abdul's UK citizenship ceremony, 23 October 2019

PLEASE HELP

I am looking for my brother Yusuf Musa Adam, and you might be able to help me.

He would be 18 years old now and was born in 2001. I haven't seen him since we were refugees in Chad.

If you have any information, please contact the publisher of this book.

Acknowledgements
Abdul Musa Adam

So many people have helped me since I was forced to flee my home 15 years ago. I would like to thank the following: Ira Muir – my today mum, Rachel, Georgia and Porsha – my today sisters, Philip Brannan, Richard and Sally Worthing-Davies and Marylin Tew, Tracy, Tad, Roxanne and Minnie for making me cakes, Helen and Michael Yeadon, Sasha Thorbek and Jane at Greatwood and the Northern Racing College for giving me my future today, Nikki Evans at Penbiddle Farm, Sister Barbara, the Harbour Project, Michael O'Hagan and Al Basti Equiworld, Aunty Elena, Uncle Philip and Christopher for my holidays in Wales, Chris Hancock – my first social worker, Swindon Children In Care Team, my American sister Karen, Halleluja Karen and Paul, Anna Lisa and Andrew Balding for sticking with me, and this country for giving me back my life in a different way. My God, Allah, who kept me alive and saved me.

Ros Wynne-Jones

I first met Abdul at the then Northern Racing College in Doncaster in the autumn of 2016. I was struck immediately by his air of calm kindness, incredible smile and clear affinity with horses. When we spoke, we realised we had been in some of the same places during some of the most traumatic times in Abdul's life. I had reported extensively from Sudan, where Abdul was born, and from the refugee camp in Chad where he lived for three years. We quickly started talking about these places – the food, the heat, the dust, the horror, and the beauty of the night sky.

Working with Abdul on this book has only deepened my admiration for him. He is an extraordinary young man, who has come through unimaginable experiences. He is only alive because somewhere deep inside him a survival instinct burns brightly, and because at almost every stage of his life someone stepped in – sometimes risking their own life – to help him because they sense his essential goodness. Next to theirs, my own contribution here is very small.

Abdul was very young through much of his journey, and there are gaps in what he remembers where the lightbulbs are literally switched off, both from trauma and just the young age he was when he was travelling. We have tried to piece together his journey as well as we can from his memories, and some of mine. I witnessed the aftermath of a massacre similar to the one that took the lives of Abdul's parents and have seen the work of the Janjaweed firsthand. So, in a sense, this is the testimony of two traumatised people. It is our truth, as close to Abdul's story as we can make it.

The story is Abdul's. But any errors in it are mine.

For my part, I would like to thank Philip Brannan for making this book happen, Jo Sollis and Fergus McKenna at Mirror Books for believing we could write it, and Reem Gabriel for acting as a gentle translator through much of the lengthy interviewing process. Thank you to my agent Laura West, at David Higham Associates, for keeping the faith, and editor George Robarts. Thank you to the Balding family, especially Anna-Lisa, for allowing me to traipse all over their beautiful backyard. Also: Ira Muir and her daughters for sharing Abdul with me, Chris Hancock for his painstaking fact-checking, and Helen Yeadon and Sasha Thorbek at Greatwood, Nikki Evans in Abergavenny, and Harriet Grant for their insight. Thank you to the inspirational Lord Alf Dubs, and to Stephen Cowan and Candida Jones.

I am also indebted to my Mirror newspaper colleagues for their patience, especially to my editor Alison Phillips and to Claire Donnelly, Clare Fitzsimons and Nick Webster, and to my writing group colleagues Nikita Lalwani and Matt Plampin for their support. Most of all, thank you to my family – Cheryl, Carmen and Rafael, and my parents Patricia and David – because writing this book has made me even more grateful every day for the riches I have.